AF840610

Priya Gopal is a barrister at Gatehouse Chambers. Her practice encompasses all aspects of Property Law, Commercial Dispute Resolution, Professional Liability and Costs. She is an experienced court advocate, appearing in trials, interim applications, appeals and hearings on ancillary matters, often against counsel who are more senior to her in call.

A Practical Guide to Easements, Restrictive Covenants and Rights of Way

A Practical Guide to Easements, Restrictive Covenants and Rights of Way

Priya Gopal

Barrister, Lincoln's Inn

LLB (Hons), LLM

Law Brief Publishing

© Priya Gopal

All rights reserved. No part of this publication may be reproduced, stored in a retrieval system, or transmitted, in any form or by any means, electronic, mechanical, photocopying, recording or otherwise, without the prior permission of the publisher.

Excerpts from judgments and statutes are Crown copyright. Any Crown Copyright material is reproduced with the permission of the Controller of OPSI and the King's Printer for Scotland. Some quotations may be licensed under the terms of the Open Government Licence (http://www.nationalarchives.gov.uk/doc/open-government-licence/version/3).

Cover image © iStockphoto.com/Drimafilm

The information in this book was believed to be correct at the time of writing. All content is for information purposes only and is not intended as legal advice. No liability is accepted by either the publisher or author for any errors or omissions (whether negligent or not) that it may contain. Professional advice should always be obtained before applying any information to particular circumstances.

Published 2023 by Law Brief Publishing, an imprint of Law Brief Publishing Ltd
30 The Parks
Minehead
Somerset
TA24 8BT

www.lawbriefpublishing.com

Paperback: 978-1-914608-71-1

PREFACE

Easements and restrictive covenants both involve limitations on a proprietor's use of their land and therefore directly impinge upon their autonomy to make free use of their land. It is therefore unsurprising that easements and restrictive covenants present a fertile ground for conflict.

This book addresses the fundamental questions of how the courts are likely to balance the competing interests of landowners, the factors the courts will consider in determining such disputes and the remedies that are available to proprietors.

It also aims to provide a tool for navigating these complex areas in practice, including guidance on evidence and procedure.

The law is as stated at 28 April 2023.

Priya Gopal
April 2023

CONTENTS

TABLE OF CASES

TABLE OF STATUTES AND PROCEDURAL RULES

CHAPTER ONE

RIGHTS OF WAY AND OTHER COMMON EASEMENTS

Where there is some disagreement about whether there is in fact an easement, the starting point is to consider the right claimed against the requirements stated in ***Re Ellenborough Park*** **[1956] Ch. 131**. In that case, the court indicated that the essential qualities of an easement are as follows:

(1) There must be a dominant and servient tenement;

(2) The easement must accommodate the dominant tenement;

(3) The dominant and servient owners must be different persons; and

(4) The right claimed must be capable of forming the subject matter of a grant.

This Chapter deals primarily with requirements (2) and (4).

It should also be noted that an easement may be characterised as positive or negative. The former typically allows the dominant proprietor to carry out some act on the servient land (such as a right of way). The latter generally involves a right to receive and may restrict the servient owner's ability to use the land (for instance a right to light).

Accommodating the dominant tenement

In ***Re Ellenborough Park***, the Court of Appeal stated that "accommodate" required the easement to be connected with the enjoyment of the dominant tenement and for its benefit. More recently in ***Regency Villas Title Ltd v Diamond Resorts (Europe) Ltd*** **[2018] UKSC 57**, the court emphasised that "accommodate" is a question of fact and should be analysed by considering whether the easement served the normal use and enjoyment of the dominant tenement. The example provided by Lord Briggs is worth repeating. He stated:

> "*Thus for example, a right granted to the owners and occupiers of a house in Kennington to have free access to the Oval cricket ground on test match days might be annexed to the ownership of that house, and add significantly to its value. But it would have nothing to do with the normal use of the property as a home*".

The following considerations will be pertinent to the question of whether a purported easement accommodates the dominant tenement:

(1) The connection between the right claimed and use of the dominant tenement, based on the facts and circumstances of the individual case;

(2) Is the benefit to the land or purely to an individual? In most cases (and indeed this was recognised in ***Regency Villas***), benefit to land may result in benefit to an individual. However, what the law of easements in this regard is seeking to guard against is a case where the right claimed is purely personal and therefore cannot be regarded as being of some practical importance to the dominant land;

(3) It is not sufficient that the right confers an advantage on the owner and/or renders ownership of the land more valuable (***Re Ellenborough Park***);

(4) Rights which involve some sort of commercial advantage to the servient land may be regarded as an easement. For example, in ***Moody v Steggles*** **(1879) 12 Ch D 261**, the proprietors of a public house claimed the right to affix a signboard to the wall of the Defendant's house. After discussing the distinction between a right which related to the land and a right which related to the business of the occupant on the land, the court concluded that the right was capable of constituting an easement. In particular, it was said that the easement claimed was "*more or less connected with the mode in which the occupant of the house uses it*". However, see ***Hill v Tupper*** **(1863) 2 Hurl & C 121** for a contrasting decision where the right to put pleasure boats for hire on a canal was not regarded as an easement, predominantly because such a right was "*unconnected with the use and enjoyment of [the] land*".

Capable of forming the subject matter of a grant

This chapter does not purport to delineate all the different forms of easements that are recognised under the law. Rather, the purpose of this chapter is to discuss the most frequently encountered easements and issues arising in practice. More generally, in ***Regency Villas***, Lord Briggs stated that:

(1) The right must not be so extensive or invasive so as to oust the servient owner from the enjoyment/control of the servient tenement; and

(2) The grant of the easement should not impose upon the servient owner an obligation to carry out management or maintenance.

Right of Way

A right of way is typically framed so as to: (1) define the land over which the right of way exists; (2) prescribe the manner in which the right of way can be exercised, for instance, it could be by foot or through vehicles; (3) prescribe the frequency of use or identify times of day when the right of way can be used; or (4) identify the purpose for which the right of way can be exercised.

With these in mind, practitioners will generally find that disputes in respect of rights of way generally (although not exclusively) fall within the following categories:

(1) A dispute may arise as to whether the right of way extends to all or part of the land identified. In this regard, Patten J in ***Perlman v Rayden*** [2004] EWHC 2192 (Ch) stated that "*it is a question of construction in every case whether a right of way gives access to each and every part of the dominant tenement or only to a particular point of access in it*". Where there is some obstruction which prevents use of the full right of way, it will be a question of construction as to whether the grant should be given a more restricted meaning. Accordingly, in ***Charles v Beach*** [1993] E.G. 124 (C.S.), Waite LJ clarified that: "*The more transient or insubstantial the obstacle, the more ready the court will be to infer that it was the intention of the grantor to over-ride the obstruction, and (conversely) the more solid and permanent the obstruction, the greater will be the reluctance of the court to impute to the grantor any intention to give the dominant owner the right to insist upon its removal*";

(2) The dominant owner may seek to use the way in a manner contrary to that which has been prescribed. It may be that the grant expressly qualifies the manner in which the easement can be used e.g. limiting to use by foot only. Alternatively, the grant may be widely drafted. In such a case, it may be that the right of way is limited by the physical characteristics of the land e.g. prohibiting use by a lorry where the dimensions would not permit this. Thus, in ***Cannon v Villars*** **(1878) 8 Ch. D. 415**, the court stated that: "*Prima facie the grant of a right of way is the grant of a right of way having regard to the nature of the road over which it is granted and the purpose for which it is intended to be used; and both those circumstances may be legitimately called in aid in determining whether it is a general right of way, or a right of way restricted to foot-passengers, or restricted to foot-passengers and horsemen or cattle, which is generally called a drift way, or a general right of way for carts, horses, carriages, and everything else*";

(3) There may be increased frequency or intensity of use. Excessive user is discussed in Chapter 3 and Extinguishment is discussed in Chapter 4. However, it is worth noting that not all increased use will be outside the scope of the easement granted. See, for example, ***British Railways Board v Glass*** [1965] Ch. 538 where the Court of Appeal concluded that the mere increase in the number of caravans using a site did not constitute a radical change in the character of the dominant tenement and so there was no excessive use;

(4) A dominant owner may seek to use the right of way for a purpose which is different to that defined by the wording of the easement or more extensive than the right acquired by prescription:

a. Where the easement was granted by deed, the analysis is likely to begin with an interpretation question, namely whether the wording of the easement is sufficient to permit the use claimed. Alternatively, for prescriptive easements, the circumstances will be assessed by reference to the right acquired;

b. The courts have generally been reluctant to permit increased use. Thus, in ***Cowling v Higginson*** **(1838) 4 Meeson and Welsby 245**, Lord Abinger stated that: "*If a way has been used for several purposes, there may be a ground for inferring that there is a right of way for all purposes; but if the evidence shews a user for one purpose, or for particular purposes only, an inference of a general right would hardly be presumed*";

c. Use that goes beyond that which was conferred or acquired is likely to be met with an argument of excessive user (for which, see Chapter 3);

(5) The grantee may seek to use the right of way to access land other than the dominant land:

a. In ***Harris v Flower*** **(1904) 74 LJ Ch 127**, Romer LJ stated that: "*If a right of way be granted for the enjoyment of close A, the grantee, because he owns or acquires close B, cannot use the way in substance for passing over close A to close B*". This rule is still a good starting point when considering whether a dominant owner is entitled to use the right of way to access land other than the dominant land;

b. In some circumstances, it may be that the grantee will be permitted access to land where this is purely ancillary to the use of the dominant land: see ***National Trust v White*** [1987] 1 W.L.R. 907 and ***Gore v Naheed*** [2017] EWCA Civ 369.

c. It will be important to consider the extent of any benefit to the non-dominant land. Where the use does not benefit the non-dominant land or only benefits the dominant land to an insubstantial extent, such use may be permitted: ***Macepark (Whittlebury) Ltd v Sargant*** [2003] EWHC 427.

As to repair and maintenance of a right of way, Longmore LJ summarised the relevant principles in ***Carter v Cole*** [2006] EWCA Civ 398:

"(1) A grantor of a right of way ("the servient owner") is under no obligation to construct the way;

(2) The grantee may enter the grantor's land for the purpose of making the grant of the right of way effective viz to construct a way which is suitable for the right granted to him ("the dominant owner"); see Newcomen v Coulson (1887) 5 ChD 133, 143 per Jessel MR;

(3) Once the way exists, the servient owner is under no obligation to maintain or repair it, see Pomfret v Ricroft (1669) 1 Wms. Saunders (1871 ed) 557 per Twysden J, Taylor v Whitehead (1781) 2 Doug KB 745 and Jones v Pritchard [1908] 1 Ch 630, 637, per Parker J;

(4) Similarly, the dominant owner has no obligation to maintain or repair the way, see Duncan v Louch (1845) 6 QB 904;

(5) The servient owner (who owns the land over which the way passes) can maintain and repair the way, if he chooses;

(6) The dominant owner (in whose interest it is that the way be kept in good repair) is entitled to maintain and repair the way and, if he wants the way to be kept in repair, must himself bear the cost: Taylor v Whitehead (1781) 2 Doug KB, per Lord Mansfield. He has a right to enter the servient owner's land for the purpose but only to do necessary work in a reasonable manner, see Liford's Case (1614) 11 Co Rep 46b, 52a (citing a case in the reign of Edward IV) and Jones v Pritchard [1908] 1 Ch 630, 638 per Parker J."

Further, in the recent decision of ***Lamport v Jones* [2023] EWHC 667 (Ch)**, Mellor J confirmed (citing ***Jones v Pritchard* [1908] 1 Ch 630**) that each party "*may do such acts on the property of the other as are reasonably necessary to the continued enjoyment of the easement*".

Right to light

A right to light may be expressly granted, it may be implied or acquired through prescription – for which see Chapter 2. The core principles to bear in mind when dealing with a right to light case can be summarised as follows:

(1) A right to light cannot exist in respect of land that has no buildings erected, namely there must be some aperture through which the right to light can be enjoyed: ***Roberts v Macord* (1832) 1 Moody and Robinson 230.**

(2) For the purpose of section 3, PA 1832, a court is unlikely to accept that a right to light has been "*actually enjoyed*" in

circumstances where panelling has been used to block the entrance of light into the building: ***Tamares (Vincent Square) Ltd v Fairpoint Properties (Vincent Square) Ltd*** [2006] **EWHC 3589 (Ch)**.

(3) There may be a requirement for expert evidence, which is likely to include what is known as a "Waldram" analysis. Such expert evidence has been regarded as "*exceedingly useful*" but not necessarily conclusive and potentially misleading: ***Fishenden v Higgs and Hill Ltd*** [1935] **All ER Rep 435**. More recently in ***Beaumont Business Centres Ltd v Florala Properties Ltd*** [2020] **EWHC 550 (Ch)**, Peter Knox QC (sitting as Deputy Judge of the High Court) accepted that there had been criticisms of the "Waldram" analysis but stated that they should not be ignored and "*have the advantage of giving one some measure of the loss of light*".

(4) Judges are likely to benefit from a site visit and this should be factored in when determining any directions and case management to trial.

Interference with rights to light is dealt with in Chapter 3.

<u>Parking</u>

It is now accepted that the right to park can constitute an easement, provided there is a dominant tenement to which the right is appurtenant: ***Moncrieff v Jamieson*** [2007] **UKHL 42**. Such a right may be provided for expressly, implied or acquired through prescription.

Where the right to park is granted expressly, disputes may fall within the following categories:

(1) What is the scope of the land over which the right to park can be exercised?

(2) Are there any limitations on how the right to park can be exercised? E.g. are there limitations on the number of cars or times of day when the right can be used?

(3) Is the right to park subject to any other qualifications?

(4) Is the right to park enjoyed jointly with others so that there is, in effect, a right to compete? For example, an easement could be framed as "*an easement to park in common with all others entitled to do so on the rear service road*": ***Montrose Court Holdings Limited v Shamash and others*** [2006] EWCA Civ 251. The fact that there may be an insufficient number of car parking spaces to accommodate all of the potential users does not in itself make the easement too vague to constitute an easement: ***Campden Hill Gate Limited v Duchess of Bedford House RTM Company Limited & Ors*** [2022] EWHC 2489.

(5) Does the servient owner have the power to make regulations? What are the terms of these regulations?

(6) Is there a right to vary?

(7) Does the grant provide for the circumstances in which the right to park can be extinguished? (see, for example, ***Saeed v Plustrade Ltd*** [2002] 2 P. & C.R. 19)

It is sometimes argued that the right to park is ancillary to a right of access. However, it should not automatically be assumed that a right of way will always include a right to park. An important question in this regard is whether the right is "*necessary for the comfortable use and enjoyment*" of the dominant land: ***Moncrieff v Jamieson***.

For general background on the approach of the courts prior to ***Moncrieff v Jamieson***, see also: ***London & Blenheim Estates Ltd v Ladbroke Retail Parks Ltd*** [1992] 1 W.L.R. 1278 and ***Batchelor v Marlow*** [2001] EWCA Civ 1051.

Other rights

(1) A right to support may be the subject matter of an easement. Such a right was described by Megarry J in ***Byard and Others v Co-operative Permanent Building Society Ltd*** (1970) 21 P. & C.R. 807 as "*a right not to have the support removed without replacement*". Some key points to note in respect of rights to support are as follows:

a. The support may come from land or other buildings: ***Lemaitre v Davis*** (1881) 19 Ch. D. 281.

b. The right to support may be acquired through prescription so long as "*the enjoyment is peaceable and without deception or concealment and so open that it must be known that some support is being enjoyed by the building*": ***Dalton v Angus*** (1881) 6 App. Cas. 740.

c. Whilst a servient owner is not required to repair the part of the building providing support, he is not entitled to remove the support "*without providing an equivalent*": ***Bond v Nottingham Corp*** [1940] Ch. 429. However, a servient owner may be considered to owe a duty of care to prevent danger to their neighbour's land arising from a lack of support due to natural causes where "*the owner or occupier knew, or was presumed to know, of the defect or condition on his land giving rise to the danger, even though he had not created it, and where* *it was reasonably foreseeable that the defect or condition would, if not remedied, cause damage to the neighbour's land*": ***Holbeck Hall Hotel Ltd. and Another v Scarborough Borough Council*** [2000] 2 W.L.R. 1396.

d. The cause of action crystallises when there is actual damage. Thus, in ***West Leigh Colliery Company Limited v Tunnicliffe & Hampson*** Limited [1908] A.C. 27, Lord Macnaghten stated that: "*The damage, not the withdrawal of support, is the cause of action*".

(2) Whilst there is no general right to prevent a neighbour from building in a manner that would alter the flow of air (***Chastey v. Ackland*** [1895] 2 Ch. 389), a right to air may exist where it is enjoyed through a "*defined aperture or channel*": ***Hunter v Canary Wharf*** [1997] 2 W.L.R. 684.

(3) The right to privacy is not protected through easements but potentially through the law of nuisance more generally: see, for example, the recent Supreme Court decision in ***Fearn and others v Board of Trustees of the Tate Gallery*** [2023] UKSC 4.

(4) In respect of recreation rights, see ***Regency Villas*** where the court recognised that the grant of purely recreational or sporting rights could be the subject matter of an easement where it genuinely accommodated the dominant tenement. This will generally be the case where "*the actual or intended use of the dominant tenement is itself recreational*".

(5) In ***Clapman v Edwards*** [1938] 2 All ER 507, the court concluded that a right to advertise was not an easement, as there was no connection in respect of user between the dominant and servient tenements.

CHAPTER TWO

CREATION OF EASEMENTS

This Chapter considers the circumstances in which easements can be acquired, namely acquisition expressly, impliedly or through long user.

EXPRESS EASEMENTS

A legal easement may be created expressly where it has been:

(1) Granted or reserved expressly;

(2) Expressly granted by virtue of section 62, Law of Property Act 1925 ("**LPA 1925**");

(3) Conferred by statute e.g. under the Access to Neighbouring Land Act 1992, the Local Government (Miscellaneous Provisions) Act 1976 etc; or

(4) Granted by will, where provision has been made for the dominant and servient tenements (owned by the testator) to be disposed of separately.

The discussion in this Chapter focuses on (1) and (2) which are more likely to be encountered in practice.

Express grant or reservation

As a general rule, an easement must be created through a deed meeting the requirements of **section 52, LPA 1925** and, in respect of registered land, should be registered in order to operate at law: **section 27(2)(d), Land Registration Act 2002.**

In respect of reservations on the sale of property, such a reservation will operate at law notwithstanding the fact that the buyer has not granted the easement by deed. Specifically, section 65, LPA 1925 provides that:

> *"(1) A reservation of a legal estate shall operate at law without any execution of the conveyance by the grantee of the legal estate out of which the reservation is made, or any regrant by him, so as to create the legal estate reserved, and so as to vest the same in possession in the person (whether being the grantor or not) for whose benefit the reservation is made.*
>
> *(2) A conveyance of a legal estate expressed to be made subject to another legal estate not in existence immediately before the date of the conveyance, shall operate as a reservation, unless a contrary intention appears".*

Section 62, LPA 1925

Sections 62(1) and 62(2) provide as follows:

> *"(1) A conveyance of land shall be deemed to include and shall by virtue of this Act operate to convey, with the land, all buildings, erections, fixtures, commons, hedges, ditches, fences, ways, waters, water-courses, liberties,*

privileges, easements, rights, and advantages whatsoever, appertaining or reputed to appertain to the land, or any part thereof, or, at the time of conveyance, demised, occupied, or enjoyed with, or reputed or known as part or parcel of or appurtenant to the land or any part thereof.

(2) A conveyance of land, having houses or other buildings thereon, shall be deemed to include and shall by virtue of this Act operate to convey, with the land, houses, or other buildings, all outhouses, erections, fixtures, cellars, areas, courts, courtyards, cisterns, sewers, gutters, drains, ways, passages, lights, watercourses, liberties, privileges, easements, rights, and advantages whatsoever, appertaining or reputed to appertain to the land, houses, or other buildings conveyed, or any of them, or any part thereof, or, at the time of conveyance, demised, occupied, or enjoyed with, or reputed or known as part or parcel of or appurtenant to, the land, houses, or other buildings conveyed, or any of them, or any part thereof."

In summary, section 62, LPA 1925 operates in the following way:

(1) It applies in the context of conveyances, which includes mortgages and leases (section 205(1)(ii), LPA 1925) but not oral tenancies (***Rye v Rye*** **[1962] A.C. 496**);

(2) It identifies what a conveyance is deemed to include, without having to set these out;

(3) It can "elevate" permissive rights into full easements.

The scope of section 62 was discussed in ***Wright v Macadam*** **[1949] 2 K.B. 744**, where the Court of Appeal was concerned with a dispute about a tenant's right to use a coal shed. The Court of Appeal observed that:

"*First, the section is not confined to rights which, as a matter of law, were so annexed or appurtenant to the property conveyed at the time of the conveyance as to make them actual legally enforceable rights. Thus, on the severance of a piece of land in common ownership, the quasi easements de facto enjoyed in respect of it by one part of the land over another will pass although, of course, as a matter of law, no man can have a right appendant or appurtenant to one part of his property exerciseable by him over the other part of his property. Secondly, the right, in order to pass, need not be one to which the owner or occupier for the time being of the land has had what may be described as a permanent title. A right enjoyed merely by permission is enough*" (p.748).

The Court of Appeal also emphasised that: (a) the right in question must be a right known to the law; and (b) section 62 would not apply where there was "*no expectation that the enjoyment of the right could be other than temporary*".

Accordingly, whilst section 62 is broadly framed, there are limitations to the rights that are capable of passing under section 62. Thus, for example:

(1) In ***Regis Property Co Ltd v Redman and Another*** [1956] 2 QB 612, the Court of Appeal held that the right to receive a supply of hot water and central heating did not pass by virtue of section 62. It was said that: "*The obligation in question involves the performance of services, and is essentially a matter of personal contract as distinct from a right, easement or privilege capable of being granted by lease or conveyance so as to pass under the general words implied by section 62*" (pp.627-628);

(2) In ***Phipps v Pears* [1965] 1 QB 76**, the court applied ***Wright v Macadam*** and held that there was no easement known to the law as an easement to be protected from the weather;

(3) In ***Anderson and Others v Bostock* [1976] Ch 312**, the court held that exclusive and unlimited grazing rights could not exist as an appurtenant right.

It is apparent from the wording of section 62 that the position is to be examined as at the "*time of conveyance*". Thus, in ***Wood v Waddington* [2015] 2 P. & C.R. 11**, the Court of Appeal confirmed that:

(1) Section 62 required the judge to make findings of fact about how the rights had been used <u>in the period leading up to the transfer</u>;

(2) The "*time of conveyance*" included a reasonable period prior to the conveyance.

<u>Expression of contrary intention</u>

Section 62(4), LPA 1925 provides that: "*This section applies only if and as far as a contrary intention is not expressed in the conveyance, and has effect subject to the terms of the conveyance and to the provisions therein contained*".

In this regard, the authorities demonstrate that:

(1) A contrary intention may be found based on the wording of the conveyance. However, in ***Gregg v Richards* [1926] Ch 521**, the conveyance described an express grant of a right of way by reference to an area coloured green on the plan (this area was four feet wide). The part coloured green was part of a wider roadway which the claimant enjoyed use of at the time of the

conveyance. The claimant succeeded in the argument that the right to use the whole width of the roadway passed under the conveyance. Thus, the effect of section 62 was to grant a right broader than what was provided for in the conveyance.

(2) Any contrary intention must be expressed with sufficient clarity: ***Wood v Waddington*** [2015] **2 P. & C.R. 11**.

(3) Contrary intention cannot be derived solely from the surrounding circumstances (***Browning v Jack*** [2021] **UKUT 307 (LC)**).

Accordingly, where the parties intend to exclude the application of section 62, it should be done clearly to avoid the risk that the wording of the conveyance is insufficient to exclude section 62.

IMPLIED EASEMENTS

Easements are most commonly implied based on:

(1) The rule in ***Wheeldon v Burrows***;

(2) Necessity; and

(3) Common intention of the parties.

The rule in *Wheeldon v Burrows*

Broadly speaking, the rule in ***Wheeldon v Burrows*** **(1879) 12 Ch 31** applies where:

(1) A proprietor disposes of part of their land;

(2) The easements are "*continuous and apparent*";

(3) The rights claimed are "*necessary to the reasonable enjoyment of the property granted*". I note that in ***Goldberg v Edwards*** **[1950] Ch 247**, the court used the words "*reasonable or convenient*" but it is unlikely that this would change the overall analysis; and

(4) The rights claimed "*have been and are at the time of the grant used by the owners of the entirety for the benefit of the part granted*".

The application of the principles derived from ***Wheeldon v Burrows*** will very much depend on the facts and circumstances of each individual case. However, the authorities which have followed and considered ***Wheeldon v Burrows*** indicate that:

(1) The rule gives effect to the intentions of the parties. Thus, it has been said that "*the law will imply a term into a contract, where, in the light of the terms of the contract and the facts known to the parties at the time of the contract, such a term would have been regarded as reasonably necessary or obvious to the parties*" (***Moncrieff and another v Jamieson and others*** **[2007] 1 WLR 2620**);

(2) The rule is based on the principle of non-derogation from grant (reiterated in ***Taurusbuild v McQue*** **[2019] UKUT 81 (LC)**) and so any analysis of whether the rule applies in an individual case should be considered with this principle in mind;

(3) Whilst "continuous" and "apparent" traditionally denoted easements that were enjoyed without any human activity (e.g. rights of light and support) rights of way are capable of being "continuous" and "apparent" for the purpose of the rule in

Wheeldon v Burrows: ***Wood v Waddington*** **[2015] 2 P. & C.R. 11**;

(4) The terms "continuous" and "apparent" suggest that there must be on the dominant or servient tenement *"a feature which would be seen on inspection and which is neither transitory nor intermittent"*: ***Ward v Kirkland*** **[1967] Ch 194**;

(5) The question of whether an easement is "apparent" is to be assessed by reference both to the physical features as well as evidence of user. The mere existence of a right of way was not sufficient: ***Linvale Investments Ltd v Walker*** **[2016] 2 P. & C.R. 12**;

(6) The proposed easement must be "*necessary*" which was not the same as "*merely reasonably or desirable*": ***Donovan v Rana*** **[2014] EWCA Civ 99**;

(7) The rights proposed to arise by virtue of the rule in ***Wheeldon v Burrows*** should not be inconsistent with the express terms of the grant: ***Millman v Ellis*** **(1996) 71 P. & C.R. 158**;

(8) The existence of an alternative access route does not necessarily prevent the rule in ***Wheeldon v Burrows*** from applying. Rather, the question to consider is whether the easement was reasonably necessary for the enjoyment of the dominant tenement and this is not the same as a test of necessity: ***Taurusbuild v McQue*** **[2019] UKUT 81 (LC)**.

Whilst section 62 would seem like the more attractive option, in that it is not necessary for the purpose of section 62 to demonstrate that the easement was necessary for the reasonable enjoyment of the land, the rule in ***Wheeldon v Burrows*** is useful in circumstances where section 62 cannot assist, for example where it has been excluded. In practice and where the facts permit, it may be possible to plead that the rights in question were acquired through the rule in ***Wheeldon v Burrows*** as an alternative to section 62.

As to implied reservations, the general position is that a reservation in favour of land retained by a grantor will not be implied. In the event that a grantor has not expressly reserved a right over the land granted, it may be possible to rely upon necessity or common intention. In ***Colquhoun v Harris*** [2010] EWHC 3963 (Ch), Jonathan Gaunt QC, sitting as a Deputy Judge of the Chancery Division summarised the legal principles to be as follows:

> "*First, the prima facie rule is that on a disposition of part of the land of the disposing party no reservation of any easement in favour of the part retained will be implied. Secondly, if the grantor intended to reserve any right over the land granted, it was his duty to reserve it expressly in the grant. Thirdly, there can, however, be exceptions to this rule. One arises where the property retained is landlocked and a case by way of necessity arises. Another exception is where the circumstances are such as to raise the necessary inference that the common intention of both parties must have been to reserve some easement to the grantor or such as to preclude the grantee from denying the right consistently with good faith. Fourth, the scope for implication is much more restricted in the case of a reservation than on a grant. One reason is that an implied reservation will tend to run counter to the express terms of the grant and therefore, derogate from it, while in the case of an implied grant the term is implied to enable the property to be used as intended and thus to fulfil the purposes of and not to derogate from the grant. Fifthly, before the inference of an intention common to both parties that the right in question should be reserved can be drawn, the party claiming the reservation must show that the facts are not reasonably consistent with any other explanation. It is not enough that they are simply*

consistent with such an explanation.... Seventh, the implication of a way of necessity does not rest upon any principle of public policy, but upon the implication to be drawn from the facts that, unless some way is implied, a parcel of land will be inaccessible...Eighth, for an easement of necessity to arise it is generally essential that the retained land will be absolutely inaccessible or useless without it...".

Necessity

Easements of necessity are generally implied where a proprietor has disposed of part of the land with the result that there is no legally enforceable way of accessing either the land disposed of or the land retained.

The question of whether an easement of necessity arises in an individual case will require a consideration of numerous factors:

(1) The fact that the right of way claimed is a more convenient means of accessing land does not mean that the party will meet the higher threshold of necessity: ***Manjang v Drammeh*** **(1990) 61 P. & C.R. 194 at 197;**

(2) If we are concerned with an argument for an implied reservation, the starting point is that any rights the grantor required over the land transferred would have been expressly reserved. It was incumbent on the grantor to establish an exception to this rule: ***Adealon International Corpn Pty Ltd v Merton London Borough Council*** **[2007] 1 WLR 1898;**

(3) Where a grantee is entitled to a right of way arising by necessity and there is more than one option available for this right of way, the grantee is entitled to only one of these (and this is to

be selected by the grantor): ***Bolton v Bolton*** **(1879) 11 Ch. D. 968;**

(4) Other realistic possibilities of access (even if not legally enforceable at the time of the grant) are relevant: ***Adealon International Corpn Pty Ltd v Merton London Borough Council*** **[2007] 1 WLR 1898;**

(5) A right to light was not implied by way of necessity in circumstances where a room in a property could not be used as a pantry but could be used for other purposes: ***Ray v Hazeldine*** **[1904] 2 Ch. 17.** The court emphasised the distinction between "*what is absolutely necessary and what is reasonably required for the enjoyment of the land or building as it stands*";

(6) A way of necessity may be implied even if the land in question is not entirely enclosed by the land of the grantor but is enclosed by the land of a third party with whom (at the date of the grant) there existed a permissive right of way, although this means of access had since been closed: ***Barry v Hasseldine*** **[1952] Ch. 835;**

(7) Where a lease of a restaurant required the lessee to comply with health regulations (including the maintenance of sufficient ventilation) but there was no suitable ventilation system installed on the premises, an easement of necessity was implied so as to allow the lessees to fix a duct on the wall of the building which belonged to the lessor: ***Wong v Beaumont Property Trust Ltd*** **[1965] 1 Q.B. 173.** The result in this case is unsurprising and a straightforward application of the principle of non-derogation from grant – the lease was granted for the purpose of a restaurant business and the absence of an adequate ventilation system would have prevented the lessees from

operating their restaurant business in accordance with the terms of the lease.

Common intention of the parties

An easement may be implied in circumstances where it would give effect to the intentions of the parties. The requirements for an implication based on common intention were helpfully summarised in ***Pwllbach Colliery Company Limited v Woodman*** [1915] **A.C.** 634, where the court stated that:

> "*The law will readily imply the grant or reservation of such easements as may be necessary to give effect to the common intention of the parties to a grant of real property, with reference to the manner or purposes in and for which the land granted or some land retained by the grantor is to be used. See Jones v. Pritchard . 18 and Lyttelton Times Co. v. Warners. But it is essential for this purpose that the parties should intend that the subject of the grant or the land retained by the grantor should be used in some definite and particular manner. It is not enough that the subject of the grant or the land retained should be intended to be used in a manner which may or may not involve this definite and particular use*" (pp.646-647).

For instance, in ***Lyttelton Times Company Limited v Warners Limited*** [1907] **A.C.** 476, the parties had agreed that A's printing house would be rebuilt with the intention that R would rent the upper floors as additional bedrooms for their adjoining hotel and A would use the ground floor as an engine house/with printing machinery in the course of their business. Thus, the parties had shared the common intention that part of the premises would be used as hotel rooms and part as a printing house. The court held that, in the absence of evidence that A had "*erected the building or established or worked their machinery and plant improperly*", no claim in nuisance could be sustained.

On the grant of a lease, there is likely to be implied an easement to use stairs, lifts and rubbish chutes where the demise would be futile without these easements: ***Liverpool City Council v Irwin*** [1976] 2 W.L.R. 562.

PRESCRIPTION

In ***Darren and Vanessa Hughes v Incumbent of the Benefice of Frampton-on-Severn, Arlingham, Saul, Fretherne & Framilode*** **[2021] UKUT 184 (LC)**, Upper Tribunal Judge Elizabeth Cooke described the law on prescription as a "*legal jungle*". It is hard to disagree. Acquisition of easements through prescription remains a difficult area to navigate. However, the starting point is that an easement may be acquired by prescription in the following ways:

(1) Under common law prescription;

(2) Pursuant to the doctrine of lost modern grant; and

(3) By virtue of the Prescription Act 1832 ("**PA 1832**").

If the facts permit, it is not uncommon for these three methods of acquisition to be pleaded in the alternative.

Common Law prescription

Under the common law, it was presumed that where the use of land as of right could be traced back to 1189 (time immemorial), acquisition by prescription would be satisfied.

The position later changed, the reasons for which were summarised by Lord Hoffmann in ***R v Oxfordshire County Council and Another, Ex parte Sunningwell Parish Council*** [2000] 1 A.C. 335 at p.350:

> *"As time went on, however, proof of lawful origin in this way became for practical purposes impossible. The evidence was not available. The judges filled the gap with another presumption. They instructed juries that if there was evidence of enjoyment for the period of living memory, they could presume that the right had existed since 1189. After the Limitation Act 1623 (21 Jac. 1, c. 16) , which fixed a 20-year period of limitation for the possessory actions such as ejectment, the judges treated 20 years' enjoyment as by analogy giving rise to the presumption of enjoyment since 1189".*

Thus, there was a presumption that user for at least 20 years could be treated as user since 1189. However, this presumption was rebuttable through evidence that the right could not have existed in 1189 e.g. through simply showing that the user could be traced to a period later than 1189.

Lost modern grant

This fictional doctrine was designed to circumvent the difficulties arising from the fact that a claim to long user based on common law prescription could be defeated by demonstrating that user could not have existed since 1189.

The presumption operates so that, where there is user for a long period (usually for at least 20 years) it is presumed that the rights were created by deed (notwithstanding the fact that the user could not be traced back to 1189) but that the deed has been lost: ***Angus v Dalton*** **(1881)**

6 App Cas 740. Thus, in ***Tehidy Minerals Ltd and another v Norman and Others* [1971] 2 Q.B. 528**, Buckley LJ stated:

> "*...where there has been upwards of 20 years' uninterrupted enjoyment of an easement, such enjoyment having the necessary qualities to fulfil the requirements of prescription, then unless, for some reason such as incapacity on the part of the person or persons who might at some time before the commencement of the 20-year period have made a grant, the existence of such a grant is impossible, the law will adopt a legal fiction that such a grant was made, in spite of any direct evidence that no such grant was in fact made*" (p.552).

The advantage of relying on the lost modern grant is that the period of 20 years use need not (unlike under the PA 1832) run to the date of the claim.

The circumstances of the case and the factual basis of the lost modern grant claim may require a party to provide clear particulars as to whether the grant was alleged to have been made before or after certain dates. For example, in ***Tremayne and Others v English Clays Lovering Pochin & Co. Ltd.* [1972] 1 WLR 657**, the claimants argued that (whilst they were concerned with a fictional grant) they required some indication of the time period so that they could adduce evidence to rebut the plea and meet the defence. The court found that they were entitled to such further particulars.

<u>PA 1832</u>

The PA 1832 introduced an additional basis upon which a prescriptive right can be asserted.

In respect of easements (other than rights to light) section 2, PA 1832 provides that:

> *"No claim which may be lawfully made at the common law, by custom, prescription, or grant, to any way or other easement, or to any watercourse, or the use of any water, to be enjoyed or derived upon, over, or from any land or water of our said lord the King, or being parcel of the duchy of Lancaster or of the duchy of Cornwall, or being the property of any ecclesiastical or lay person, or body corporate, when such way or other matter as herein last before mentioned shall have been actually enjoyed by any person claiming right thereto without interruption for the full period of twenty years, shall be defeated or destroyed by showing only that such way or other matter was first enjoyed at any time prior to such period of twenty years, but nevertheless such claim may be defeated in any other way by which the same is now liable to be defeated; and where such way or other matter as herein last before mentioned shall have been so enjoyed as aforesaid for the full period of forty years, the right thereto shall be deemed absolute and indefeasible, unless it shall appear that the same was enjoyed by some consent or agreement expressly given or made for that purpose by deed or writing."*

Accordingly, section 2 introduces two time periods:

(1) Where there has been user as of right and without interruption for 20 years, this constitutes a defence to the argument that the user commenced after 1189; and

(2) User as of right and without interruption for 40 years renders the right "*absolute and infeasible*" unless the user was pursuant to some written consent or agreement.

Separate provision is made under section 3, PA 1832 for rights to light:

> "*When the access and use of light to and for any dwelling house, workshop, or other building shall have been actually enjoyed therewith for the full period of twenty years without interruption, the right thereto shall be deemed absolute and indefeasible, any local usage or custom to the contrary notwithstanding, unless it shall appear that the same was enjoyed by some consent or agreement expressly made or given for that purpose by deed or writing*".

Section 4, PA 1832 provides that:

> "*Each of the respective periods of years herein-before mentioned shall be deemed and taken to be the period next before some suit or action wherein the claim or matter to which such period may relate shall have been or shall be brought into question and that no act or other matter shall be deemed to be an interruption, within the meaning of this statute, unless the same shall have been or shall be submitted to or acquiesced in for one year after the party interrupted shall have had or shall have notice thereof, and of the person making or authorizing the same to be made*".

The key points arising from this section (and related case law) are as follows:

(1) The words "*next before some suit or action*" indicate that the user must be for a period of 20 years immediately before the claim is brought. Further, until the claim is brought, there can be no right to an easement.

(2) Where there has been some form of interference in respect of the easement <u>and</u> the dominant owner has acquiesced in and/or submitted to this interference for one year, this is likely to defeat a claim under the PA 1832. In order to demonstrate

acquiescence/submission, the dominant owner must have had notice of the interruption and notice of the person making/authorising the interruption: see Fry J in ***Seddon v Bank of Bolton*** **(1882) 19 Ch. D. 462** at p.464.

(3) An "interruption" connotes something more than simply non-user. Therefore, in ***Smith v Baxter*** **[1900] 2 Ch 138**, Stirling J concluded that, for the purpose of section 4, PA 1832 (and also section 3) interference "*refers to an adverse obstruction, and not to a mere discontinuance of user*".

The "user" requirements

A party must also demonstrate that there has been user of the right kind in order to acquire an easement through prescription. With the exception of rights of light acquired under section 3, PA 1832, it is necessary to show that there is use "as of right". Under the common law, this requires the user to be nec vi, nec clam and nec precario, namely without force, without secrecy and without permission.

In respect of user, the authorities indicate as follows:

(1) The use claimed must be "*of sufficient intensity or frequency to indicate that a right is being asserted*". However, the court should not require arbitrary standards of frequency. Instead, it is important to consider whether there is "*sufficient use to put the servient owner on notice that a right is being asserted and that he or she needs to take action*" (***Darren and Vanessa Hughes v Incumbent of the Benefice of Frampton-on-Severn, Arlingham, Saul, Fretherne & Framilode*** **[2021] UKUT 184 (LC)** at [18] and [25]);

(2) Where user is initially granted by a licence but that licence lapses, any subsequent occupation is unlikely to be regarded as

permissive: ***London Tara Hotel Ltd v Kensington Close Hotel Ltd*** [2011] EWCA Civ 1356;

(3) Where a car park (owned by the proprietors of club premises) had signs erected stating that the car park was private and for use of club patrons only, use of that car park by the operators of an adjacent fish shop could not be "as of right". Specifically, the presence of the signs were sufficient for a landowner to indicate that they did not acquiesce in the unlawful user (***Winterburn and another v Bennett and another*** [2017] 1 W.L.R. 646). Further, in ***Winterburn***, the court considered the meaning of "*without force*". It was said that:

   a. "*The phrase "without force" carries rather more than its literal meaning. It is not enough for the person asserting the right to show that he has not used violence. He must show that his user was not contentious or allowed only under protest...*" [13];

   b. "*...the authorities do not support the proposition that a servient owner must be prepared to back his objection either by physical obstruction or by legal action or the proposition that the servient owner is required to do everything, proportionately to the user, to contest and to endeavour to interrupt the user*" [36];

(4) Use may be regarded as secretive "*if the identity of the person enjoying the use is unknown to the owner of the putative servient land*": see ***London Tara Hotel Ltd v Kensington Close Hotel Ltd*** [2011] EWCA Civ 1356 at [35];

(5) In ***R. (on the application of Beresford) v Sunderland City Council*** [2003] UKHL 60, the House of Lords emphasised that:

a. A licence cannot be implied simply because there has been "*inaction of a landowner with knowledge of the use to which his land is being put*" [6];

b. The act of giving permission may be informal but must "*involve a positive act of granting the use of the property, as opposed to mere acquiescence in its use*" [57];

c. Permission is established where there is: "*a communication by some overt act which is intended to be understood, and is understood, as permission to do something which would otherwise be an act of trespass*" [75];

d. The law would not "*treat a landowner's silent passive acquiescence in persons using his land as having the same effect as permission communicated (whether in writing, by spoken words, or by overt and unequivocal conduct) to those persons*" [79].

It should be noted that some of the reasoning adopted in this decision was regarded as incorrect by the House of Lords in ***R. (on the application of Barkas) v North Yorkshire CC*** [2014] UKSC 31 but not in respect of the specific points summarised in these paragraphs.

(6) The legal burden of proving that the use was "as of right" is on the party claiming the easement: see, for example, ***Welford v Graham*** [2017] UKUT 297 (TCC) which also includes a useful discussion on evidential presumptions.

As to user under the PA 1832, section 5 indicates that: "*it shall be sufficient to allege the enjoyment thereof* ***<u>as of right</u>*** *by the occupiers of the tenement in respect whereof the same is claimed*" (emphasis added). In ***Gardner v. Hodgson's Kingston Brewery Co. Ltd.*** [1903] A.C. 229

Lord Lindley stipulated that the words "as of right" were intended to be a reference to nec vi, nec clam, nec precario.

CHAPTER THREE

EASEMENTS AND LIABILITY

INTERFERENCE

A claim for the interference or infringement of an easement is brought through an action in private nuisance. In order to bring such a claim, a claimant would generally need to demonstrate:

(1) That they are entitled to and/or have acquired the easement (see Chapter 2 on creation of easements);

(2) The ambit and extent of the easement; and

(3) Substantial interference of the right claimed.

Ambit and extent of the easement

The question of scope is usually determined by reference to the method of acquisition of an easement.

Accordingly, where we are concerned with an express easement, the scope of such an easement will be a matter of interpretation, with the analysis being conducted using the well-established principles of construction. A useful summary of the approach to be taken was provided by O'Farrell J in ***2 Entertain Video Limited v Sony DADC Europe Limited*** [2020] EWHC 972 (TCC) at [221]:

> "*The applicable legal principles of contract construction are well-established. When interpreting a written contract, the court's task is to ascertain the objective meaning of the language which the parties have chosen to express their agreement. It does so, having regard to the meaning of the relevant words in their documentary, factual and commercial context. That meaning has to be assessed in the light of:*
>
> *(i) the natural and ordinary meaning of the clause;*
>
> *(ii) any other relevant provisions of the contract;*
>
> *(iii) the overall purpose of the clause and the contract;*
>
> *(iv) the facts and circumstances known or assumed by the parties at the time that the document was executed; and*
>
> *(v) commercial common sense; but*
>
> *(vi) disregarding subjective evidence of any party's intentions*".

In ***Shaw v Peter David Grouby, Claude Anthony Francis Barkham* [2017] EWCA Civ 233**, the court was concerned with a right of way framed in the following terms:

> "*To pass and repass at all times and for all purposes over and along so much of the private driveway edged green on the said plan as is necessary to obtain access to the Property subject to the proviso that the Buyers shall contribute a fair and reasonable proportion of the cost of maintaining the same in a good and sufficient state of repair according to the extent of the user of the driveway by the Buyers*".

One of the issues for the court to determine was whether the word "necessary" required the beneficiary of the easement to use the shortest route possible. The Court of Appeal concluded that it did not. Further, "necessary" was not to be determined by reference to a fixed point in time. The grant did not limit the right of way to a fixed point of access. It is apparent from the judgment of the Court of Appeal that the nature and extent of an express grant is likely to be determined by reference to (inter alia):

(1) The wording of the grant;

(2) The other words of a transfer or conveyance, for example if there is a cost-contribution clause; and

(3) Any plans referred to in the grant and the stated purpose of the plans.

In respect of implied easements and/or easements acquired through prescription, there will of course be a greater focus on how the easement has been used in practice.

It is also important to establish the limitations or restrictions which emanate from the grant of the easement. Specifically, there may be a limitation on how much of the servient land the easement extends to. Additionally, there may be restrictions on purpose or the nature of use. In each case, the nature and extent of any limitations will be a question of fact. Thus, whilst the case law provides us with some assistance, even where (when looked at superficially) the wording of the easements in two separate cases are the same, the circumstances may lead to disparate results.

Substantial interference of the right claimed

General

As to what constitutes an actionable interference with an easement, the authorities indicate as follows:

(1) It is not sufficient to demonstrate that there has been an interference with an easement. Rather, it is necessary to show that the interference is "substantial". An interference is not actionable if the right/easement "*can be substantially and practically exercised as conveniently after as before the occurrence of the alleged obstruction*" (***West v Sharp*** **(2000) 79 P. & C.R. 327** at p.332);

(2) An interference is unlikely to be regarded as substantial if it does not interfere with the reasonable use of a right of way (***Celsteel Limited v. Alton House Limited*** **[1985] 1 W.L.R. 204** at p. 217);

(3) In ***B&Q plc v Liverpool & Lancashire Properties Ltd*** **[2000] EWHC 463 (Ch)**, Blackburne J stated (in the context of a right of way dispute) that:

a. The question is not "*whether what the grantee is left with is reasonable, but whether his insistence on being able to continue the use of the whole of what he contracted for is reasonable*" [45];

b. "*…it is not open to the grantor to deprive the grantee of his preferred modus operandi and then argue that someone else would prefer to do things differently, unless the grantee's preference is unreasonable or perverse*" [45];

c. Where a grantee has contracted for what was described as an "ample right", he should not be deprived of this right simply because it was a luxury and the "*reduced, non-ample right would be all that was reasonably required. The test was one of convenience and not necessity or reasonable necessity*" [47];

d. The fact that an interference may be regarded as "infrequent" or "fleeting" does not mean that the interference is not substantial [73];

(4) Whether there has been a substantial interference with an easement is a question of fact. Accordingly, the presence of a lock may constitute a substantial interference in one case (***Dickinson v Cassillas*** [2017] **EWCA Civ 1254**) but not in another (***Dawes v Adela Estates Ltd*** **(1970) 216 E.G. 1405**).

Right to light

An interference with a right to light is treated differently. In particular, a claimant cannot succeed in an action simply by showing that the amount of light enjoyed is less than before. Rather, it is necessary to demonstrate that the infringement amounts to a nuisance. In ***Colls v Home & Colonial Stores Ltd*** [1904] **A.C. 179**, Lord Macnaghten expressed the position in the following terms:

> "*It was not sufficient to constitute an illegal obstruction, that the plaintiff had, in fact, less light than before; nor does his warehouse, the part of his house principally affected, could not be used for all the purposes to which it might otherwise have been applied. In order to give a right of action and sustain the issue, there must be a substantial privation of light, sufficient to render the occupation of the house uncomfortable, and to*

prevent the plaintiff from carrying on his accustomed business (that of a grocer) on the premises as beneficially as he had formally done" (p.187).

Additionally, in ***Carr-Saunders v Dick McNeil Associates Ltd*** **[1986] 1 W.L.R. 922**, Millett J provided the following guidance in respect of interference with the right to light:

(1) There can be no actionable wrong if the amount of light that remained was sufficient for "*the comfortable enjoyment of his property by the dominant owner according to the ordinary notions of mankind*" (p.928);

(2) The focus should not be on the amount of light taken but instead to the amount of light left (p.928). This principle was re-iterated in ***Higgins v Betts*** **[1905] 2 Ch 210**, where Farwell J indicated that the focus is on the light remaining and not on how much has been taken away, namely: "*the test is not whether so much light has been taken as materially to lessen the enjoyment and use of the house that its owner previously had, but whether so much is left as is enough for the comfortable use and enjoyment of the house according to the ordinary requirements of mankind*".

(3) "*the dominant owner's right of light is not measured by the particular use to which the dominant tenement has been put in the past... The extent of the dominant owner's right is neither increased nor diminished by the actual use to which the dominant owner has chosen to put his premises or any of the rooms in them: for he is entitled to such access of light as will leave his premises adequately lit for all ordinary purposes for which they may reasonably be expected to be used. The court must, therefore, take account not only of the present use, but also of other potential uses to which the dominant owner may reasonably be expected to put the premises in the future*" (p.928).

The question of interference is, of course, to be measured by the property in question. Thus, the amount of light to be expected in a warehouse would be very different from the light one might expect in a greenhouse: ***Allen v Greenwood*** [1980] Ch. 119.

The court is permitted to have regard to the locality of the property when assessing whether the test for interference has been satisfied: ***Ough v King*** [1967] 1 W.L.R. 1547.

Where the dominant owner has access to other sources of light (i.e. sources of light which he/she is entitled to) these should be taken into account in determining the question of interference: ***Smith v Evangelization Society (Incorporated) Trust*** [1933] Ch. 515.

Landlord's right to develop

The question of whether there has been a substantial interference can be particularly complex where: (1) a landlord has granted an easement to a tenant; and (2) the landlord has reserved a right to develop in a lease, a fairly common clause. Where a landlord seeks to redevelop, this creates a tension between the right to develop and a tenant's right to an easement. As such, whilst there may be an argument that the tenant's right to develop is qualified by the landlord's right to develop, a court is unlikely to allow a landlord to simply ignore an easement or allow the easement to essentially be reduced to nothingness (see, for example, ***Overcom Properties v. Stockleigh Hall Residents Management Ltd*** (1988) 58 P. & C.R. 1). That being said, where a landlord carries out acts of development which could amount to an infringement in ordinary circumstances, this should be viewed in the context of the landlord's right to develop.

Some examples of how the courts have resolved this tension are provided below:

(1) Where a landlord granted a lease of a unit in a shopping precinct with a specified intended purpose for the centre but reserving to the landlord the right to build, rebuild or alter "*notwithstanding that the access of light or air to the Premises may be obstructed diminished or interfered with or that any other liberty privilege easement quasi-easement right benefit or advantage now or from time to time appertaining to or reputed to appertain to or enjoyed or intended to be enjoyed by the Premises or by the Tenant is thereby diminished or prejudicially affected*", the landlord was under an obligation to ensure that he did not alter or use the common parts in such a manner that it would lose its character as a retail shopping mall (***Petra Investments Ltd v Jeffrey Rogers Plc*** (2001) **81 P. & C.R. 21**);

(2) In circumstances where a landlord granted a right to park to a tenant (and various other people) but then carried out works which reduced the availability of parking spaces from 12/13 spaces to 4 spaces, this constituted a substantial interference and a clear derogation from the right to park conferred (***Saeed v Plustrade Ltd*** [2001] **EWCA Civ 2011**);

(3) In ***Platt and Others v London Underground Ltd*** [2001] 2 **E.G.L.R. 121**, a lease was granted in respect of two kiosks at Goodge Street Underground Station. The lease included a clause which provided that: "*Notwithstanding anything herein contained, the lessee shall not be entitled to raise any objection in respect of the construction, working, or carrying on by the Company of its present or any future undertaking or works, or any part thereof, or anything arising therefrom in respect of any buildings, erections, or works, which now or may be built, erected, or constructed by the Company over, under, adjoining, or near to the demise premises, or the construction, erection, or use thereof, respectively, and the Company shall not be responsible to the lessee either under these present or under any public or private statute or*

at common law for any damage, injury, annoyance or inconvenience, howsoever caused, which may arise in consequence of or in relation to the said buildings, erections, or works, or the working or carrying on by the Company of its present or any future undertaking of works". In relation to one of the kiosks, the relevant exit did not open outside the morning rush hours and the Claimant contended that this deprived them of a substantial portion of their potential trade. The court accepted that this amounted to a derogation from grant. However, when considering remedies, the court stated that it was entitled to take into account any increased profits made at the other kiosk by way of set off.

EXCESSIVE USER

Liability may arise in trespass (***Bracewell v Appleby*** [1975] Ch. 408) or nuisance (***McAdams Homes Ltd v Robinson*** [2004] EWCA Civ 214) where there has been excessive use of an easement, namely the use goes beyond the rights which were granted or acquired.

It will of course be necessary to determine the ambit and extent of the easement before considering whether there is any excessive user.

Whether the given circumstances of a case present "excessive use" is a question of fact and degree (***Bucknell v Alchemy Estates (Holywell) Ltd (No.2)*** [2023] EWHC 683 (Ch)). However, excessive use may be found to exist where there is increased user or user for a different purpose. For example:

(1) Where the conveyance of part of a large agricultural estate granted "*the right of way at all times and for all purposes over the driveway ... leading to the main road, in common with all other persons having the like right*", the use of the driveway for the

purpose of accessing a caravan site amounted to excessive user (***Jelbert v Davis and Another*** **[1968] 1 W.L.R. 589**). In ***Jelbert***, the court further confirmed that the person with the benefit of a right of way should not use it "*to an extent which is beyond anything which was contemplated at the time of the grant*";

(2) In ***White and Another v Richards*** **[1993] R.T.R. 318**, the conveyance conferred the right (in respect of agricultural land) to the benefit of a "*right...at all times hereafter to pass and repass on foot and with or without motor vehicles*" along circa 250 metres of track. The primary question for the court was whether use was restricted by the physical characteristics of the way. The judge found that, the defendant's use (which sometimes involved travelling along the track with 14 heavy lorries a day) constituted excessive use. Further, it was proper of the judge to restrict the size/type of the vehicle by reference to the physical characteristics of the track;

(3) In ***Mills v Partridge*** **[2020] EWHC 2171 (Ch)**, a conveyance provided that use of a right of way was to be "*for all purposes in connection with the use of the land ... as agricultural land only...*". The right of way was originally to a nursery but the nursey business had since expanded over time into a business that included polytunnels, a licensed tea room, retail area and car park. In concluding that the use had steered beyond agricultural use, Judge Simon Barker QC observed that:

a. There was a distinction to be drawn between developments in agricultural practices and diversification into non-agricultural activity **[71]**;

b. A restriction on use as "agricultural land" would not be breached by use which is <u>incidental</u> to the agricultural use **[83]**;

c. "*The tea room has a different character and purpose from the Nursery, its physical integration into the Nursery does not render it incidental or ancillary to the Nursery, and its addition to the Nursery impacts significantly on the view to be taken of the Nursery as a whole*" [**111**].

See also Chapter 1 for a discussion on excessive user in respect of specific easements.

Where excessive user is established, a court is likely to grant an injunction to restrain this. However, see Chapter 4 for a discussion on extinguishment and alteration.

CHAPTER FOUR

EXTINGUISHMENT OF EASEMENTS

Broadly speaking, an easement can be extinguished through:

(1) Express release

(2) Implied release

(3) Operation of law

(4) Statute

Express release

For an express release to take effect at law, it should be carried out by deed. It is, of course, advisable, for any such express release to clearly identify (inter alia) the terms of the release, including the rights which are being released and the position of any mortgagees.

Where no deed has been used but the agreement complies with the requirements of section 2, Law of Property (Miscellaneous Provisions) Act 1989, a party may be able to rely on estoppel, namely to argue that the other party is estopped from denying the release. The difficulties with this argument (where the property is transferred to a third party) were clearly demonstrated in ***Allen and another v Jones and another*** [2004] EWHC 1119 (QB). In that case, the dominant land was sold before the agreement to release could be incorporated into a deed. The court concluded that any extinguishment argument vis-à-vis the third party purchasers who did not have notice of the agreement did not "*get beyond first base*" [28].

Implied release

Abandonment

The ultimate question in each case is whether the facts and circumstances demonstrate an intention to abandon. Thus, in ***Gotobed v Pridmore*** (1971) 217 E.G. 759, Buckley LJ stated: "*To establish abandonment of an easement the conduct of the dominant owner must, in their Lordships' judgment, have been such as to make it clear that he had at the relevant time a firm intention that neither he nor any successor in title of his should thereafter make use of the easement*".

Although, to an extent, the analysis differs depending on whether we are concerned with continuous easements (e.g. a right to light) or discontinuous easements (e.g. a right of way), they are (arguably) simply different methods of resolving the same question: is there an intention to abandon?

Moore v Rawson (1824) 3 B. & C. 332 provides an example of abandonment in the context of a continuous easement. In that case, the dominant land originally benefited from a right to light through an ancient window of a house. The house was then pulled down and a blank wall was erected instead, without windows. This continued for circa 17 years. The servient owner erected a building opposite the dominant owner's blank wall. The dominant owner then opened a window within the blank wall and contended that the servient owner had infringed his right to light. The court dismissed the claim. Lord Abbott CJ also emphasised that the burden was on the dominant owner to show that when he abandoned the windows, this was "*not a perpetual, but a temporary abandonment of the enjoyment*".

Conversely, the decision in *Ecclesiastical Commissioners v Kino* **(1880) 14 Ch. D. 213** demonstrates that the fact of pulling down a building that benefited from a right to light was not in itself sufficient to establish abandonment. James LJ considered whether there was evidence that the dominant owner was "*about to restore the building with its ancient lights*" (page 219).

In the context of discontinuous easements, the primary argument which is made in practice is non-user. The authorities establish that non-user does not, in itself, constitute abandonment:

(1) A presumption of abandonment cannot be made from the fact of non-user: ***Ward v Ward*** **(1852) 7 Ex 838**;

(2) A lengthy period of non-user does not extinguish an easement (without more): ***Hall v Swift*** **(1838) 4 Bingham New Cases 381**;

(3) Non-user of a right of way may be justified by the fact that there was an alternative, more convenient route. This does not mean that there is an intention to abandon in respect of the original route: ***Williams v Sandy Lane (Chester) Ltd*** **[2007] 1 P. & C.R. 27**;

(4) Where there is non-user, this should be considered in conjunction with the surrounding circumstances to determine whether there is abandonment: ***Swan v. Sinclair*** **[1924] 1 Ch. 254**;

(5) It must also be shown that the owner of the dominant land had a fixed intention never, at any time in the future, to assert the right to the easement or to attempt to transmit it to someone else: ***Tehidy Minerals Ltd v Norman*** **[1971] 2 QB 528**;

(6) In ***Dwyer v Westminster CC*** **[2014] 2 P & CR 7**, the court confirmed that abandonment was not a subjective question and not something to be lightly inferred;

(7) More recently in ***Annetts v Adeleye*** **[2018] EWCA Civ 555**, the Court of Appeal confirmed that the test was one of the "*reasonable perception of the servient owner and what he would conclude as to the dominant owner's intentions*".

The dominant owner may also be estopped from claiming the right to an easement in circumstances where, for example, they allow and/or encourage others to expend sums on the basis of the right not being used. Accordingly, in ***Lester v Woodgate*** **[2010] EWCA Civ 199**, the court stated that: "*If the claimant's conduct at the time takes the form of encouraging the defendant to believe that his otherwise tortious interference with the claimant's property will be waived and not objected to and, in reliance on that, the defendant subsequently acts in a way which can be characterised as detrimental then the position is, I think, different from the facts considered in Ramsden v Dyson and the court does then have to decide whether the causative effect of that conduct is sufficient to bar the enforcement of the legal right*".

Alteration

Where the use that the dominant land is put to is altered, the question arises whether this amounts to extinguishment of an easement.

In determining whether the alteration constitutes extinguishment, a court is likely to have regard to the following factors:

(1) The prejudice caused to the proprietor of the servient land: ***Saunders v Newman*** **(1818) 1 Barn. & Ald. 258**;

(2) Whether the alteration was minor: ***Hall v Swift*** **(1838) 4 Bing. N.C. 381** (arguably, this is connected with the overall consideration of prejudice);

(3) Any increased burden caused by the altered use: ***RPC Holdings v Rogers*** **[1953] 1 All E.R. 1029**; and

(4) Whether the development of the dominant land represented a "radical change in the character" or a "change in the identity" of the land and whether the use of the land as redeveloped would result in a substantial increase or alteration in the burden on the servient land: ***McAdams Homes Ltd v Robinson*** **[2005] 1 P. & C.R. 30**.

Note that alteration could also simply lead to suspension of the easement rather than extinguishment.

Operation of law

Unity of possession

Where both possession and ownership of the freehold estates in respect of the dominant and servient tenements vest in the same person, an easement will be extinguished. It is therefore insufficient (for the purpose of extinguishment) to have unity of possession without a unity of ownership: ***Canham v Fisk*** **(1831) 2 Cr & J 126**.

Accordingly, in ***Thomas v Thomas*** **(1835) 2 C.M. & R. 34**, Alderson B summarised the position to be as follows:

> *"If I am seised of freehold premises, and possessed of leasehold premises adjoining, and there has formerly been an easement enjoyed by the occupiers of the one as against the occupiers of the other, while the premises are in my hands, the easement is*

> *necessarily **suspended**, but it is not extinguished, because there is no unity of seisin; and if I part with the premises, the right, not being extinguished, will revive*" (page 41, emphasis added).

Similarly, in ***Simper v Foley*** (1862) 2 **J. & H. 555**, the court confirmed that a "*union of the ownership of dominant and servient tenements for different estates does not extinguish an easement of this description, but merely suspends it so long as the union of ownership continues, and upon a severance of the ownership the easement revives*".

It is therefore important to consider, in the individual case, whether what may appear as extinguishment is in fact purely a suspension of the easement. The distinction, of course, has significant implications.

Merger

In ***Wall v Collins*** [2007] **EWCA Civ 444**, the Court of Appeal considered the position where a leasehold estate (pursuant to which the easement was granted) merged with a freehold estate. The court concluded that:

(1) Whilst an easement must be appurtenant to a dominant tenement it did not have to be appurtenant to any particular interest [15];

(2) The merger of the lease was not in itself fatal to the continued existence of the easement, for the period for which it was granted [16].

As to registration, it should be noted that (in respect of registered land) HM Land Registry will not enter the benefit of the easement automatically on the title to the reversionary estate and an application will need to be lodged: see **HM Land Registry Practice Guide 26, paragraph 3.4.**

Statute

The circumstances in which an easement may be extinguished by statute are limited and unlikely to be encountered frequently in practice. Accordingly, this Chapter does not cover extinguishment by statute in any great length and readers should consult, for example, ***Gale on Easements*** for more specific guidance on the circumstances in which an easement may be extinguished by statute.

It should be noted that extinguishment by statute does not mean a regime which allows for modification or discharge (as is the case for restrictive covenants): see Chapter 7. Rather, it refers to a situation where a statute expressly provides for extinguishment or where extinguishment arises from statutory powers, most commonly in the context of compulsory purchase.

CHAPTER FIVE

COMMON FREEHOLD COVENANTS

This chapter addresses the most common freehold covenants that practitioners are likely to encounter.

Use as a single private dwelling house and restrictions on trade

Conveyances (particularly in the context of an estate that has been developed) often include a covenant which requires a property to be used only as a single private dwelling-house. This is usually accompanied by a covenant which prohibits use of the property as a trade or business. Provisions to this effect may be framed in the following terms:

> "*...not to use or permit to be used the property for any purpose other than that of a private dwelling house and no trade or business or manufacture of any kind shall at any time be permitted to be set up or carried on on any part of the property or in any building now or hereafter within the perpetuity period erected thereon*".

Such a covenant may be breached through taking in paying guests and visitors, often by way of short-term occupation.

Taking in friends and others as paying guests in order to meet rent, rates and outgoings is likely to be regarded as a breach of covenant (*Thorn v Madden* [1925] Ch. 847). In *Thorn v Madden*, Tomlin J confirmed that: (a) the court would not consider questions of hardship or housing shortages; (b) where a proprietor allows for visitors to come and live in the property "*for short or long periods upon payment for board and residence*", it could not be said that the property was being used a private residence; (c) a house which was "*permanently available for the accommodation of any approved person*" is likely to amount to the carrying on of a business.

In *C & G Homes Ltd v Secretary of State for Health* [1991] 2 All ER 841, the Secretary of State had purchased two properties for use as supervised housing for former hospital patients who had suffered from mental disabilities. The Court of Appeal held that the proposed use was not incidental to the enjoyment of a private dwelling-house. Nourse LJ considered the authorities and indicated that the question of fact and degree to be answered in each case will involve a consideration of (inter alia): "*the number of occupants; the degree of permanence of their occupancy; the relationship between them; whether payment is made or not and, if so, whether it is only a contribution to expenses or something more; whether the owner or lessee resides there himself and, if not, whether he has people there to supervise and support those who do*".

In *Caradon DC v Paton* (2001) 33 H.L.R. 34, the occupants were tenants, but holding tenancies for very short periods. Latham LJ emphasised the importance of considering the context within which the covenant was imposed. Further, he indicated that a person who is in a holiday property for a week or two would not describe that as his or her home. A degree of permanence is required in order to amount to use of a property as a home.

In *Nemcova v Fairfield Rents Ltd* [2016] UKUT 303 (LC), a long lease included a covenant stating that the demised premises were not to be used (inter alia) "*other than as a private residence*". The tribunal held that the covenant had been breached by granting a series of short-term lettings. The lessees' appeal to the Upper Tribunal was dismissed. In his judgment HHJ Stuart Bridge stated that:

a. Whilst a person may have more than one residence, it was necessary that there be "*a connection between the occupier and the residence such that the occupier would think of it as his or her residence albeit not without limit of time*"; and

b. The duration of an occupier's occupation is material. Further, there must be a degree of permanence. Thus, where a person occupies for a matter of days and then leaves, it cannot be said that use of the property is for his/her private residence.

In *Triplerose Limited v Beattie* [2020] UKUT 180, the lessee covenanted "*Not at any time to carry on or permit to be carried on upon the Property any trade or business whatsoever nor to use or permit the same to be used for any purpose other than as a private dwelling house for occupation by one family at any one time*'. The lessees arranged for their flat to be advertised on the Airbnb and Booking.com as available to let for short term occupation, although the lessees still made regular use of it. The Upper Tribunal concluded that the lessees were in breach of covenant. Martin Rodger QC stated that: "*the use of residential property for short term occupation by a succession of paying guests has always been treated as a breach of a covenant requiring use only as a private residence or dwellinghouse*".

In respect of the "trade or business" prohibition, a distinction needs to be drawn between the situation where there is a total prohibition or where the covenant in question limits use of the property to a particular "trade or business". Further, practitioners may be concerned with a clause which limits use to trade or business A and the question in the individual case may be whether the proprietor, in carrying out trade or business B is in breach. Some examples of the application of such "trade or business" clauses is provided below:

(1) Where a covenant prohibits the use of property as a cinema, use as a means of access to land used for both retail and a cinema would not necessarily be regarded as a breach: ***GLN (Copenhagen) Southern Ltd v Tunbridge Wells Borough Council*** [2004] **EWCA Civ 1279**;

(2) A covenant may limit the use of the premises to the following: "*the trade or business of a grocery and general stores (which term shall not include a footwear repair service and collection centre Dry Cleaning and Laundry service Ladies Hairdressing Meat Purveyor Pharmaceutical Chemist or Newsagents Sugar Confectioner Tobacconist or Post Office)*". Operation of premises as a general store may permit the sale of tobacco. However, where the extent of what was being offered for sale was sufficient in scale to amount to a distinct trade or business, the covenant would be breached: ***Williams v Christopher Reeves Kiley (Trading as CK Supermarkets)*** [2004] **EWCA Civ 870**;

(3) The proprietors of a row of shops covenanted that they would not allow adjoining/adjacent premises to be used for the sale of tobacco, cigars and cigarettes. The adjoining premises was a tea-shop company which sold cigarettes at the cashier's desk. The court concluded that sale as an incidental part of the business of a tea shop was not a breach: ***A. Lewis and Company (Westminster), Limited v Bell Property Trust, Limited*** [1940] **Ch. 345**.

The recent decision in ***Hodgson v Cook*** [2023] **UKUT 41 (LC)** provides some useful guidance on the circumstances in which there would be a breach of the covenant not to use premises for trade or business. The covenant in question stated that: "*No trade business or profession shall be carried out upon the plot and the plot shall not be used for any other purpose other than as one private dwelling*". The applicants applied for modification of this covenant covenant on the basis that they wished to continue operating a beauty therapy business from a cabin in the rear garden. In interpreting this covenant, Mr Mark Higgin FRICS observed as follows:

"*In my view the covenant was not intended to prevent owners from occasionally working from home, alone on a laptop in a spare room. I do not regard such activity as being in conflict with the covenant and for that matter, it does not in my view, offend the second limb of the covenant that the plot should not be used for any other purpose that as one private dwelling. A covenant against carrying on a trade, business or profession in a residential property does not prohibit all activity with a commercial purpose and tasks which are consistent with ordinary residential use which are undertaken in connection with a business which is mainly carried on elsewhere are unlikely to be a breach. It is not necessary to decide where the dividing line should be drawn between conducting a business from home and occasionally working from home, because in this case there is no doubt that the whole of Mrs Hodgson's business is now conducted from the cabin in her garden, and from nowhere else. It follows that her continued use of the cabin for that purpose is impeded by the covenant*".

Covenants against building

A conveyance may include a covenant against building or construction. Such a restriction may be absolute or permitted where the stipulated conditions have been complied with. The latter situation is considered in more detail below under the heading "**Covenants requiring consent**".

The covenant may specifically restrict building. Alternatively, the argument against building may be premised on the prohibition on using the property in question other than as "*a private dwelling house*". The argument often pursued is that the article "*a*" limits the number of buildings which can be constructed. Such an argument was considered by Neuberger J in ***Crest Nicholson Residential (South) Limited v Fiona Ruth McAllister*** [2002]EWHC 2443 (Ch). In delivering judgment, Neuberger J stated that: "*the indefinite article "a" tends to carry with it the concept of singularity as opposed to plurality. Restriction to use as "a private dwelling house" appears to me, at least in the absence of contextual or factual contra-indications, to mean restriction to a single dwelling house*".

It should be noted that this decision was overturned on appeal but the appeal was decided on different grounds. However, Chadwick LJ noted Neuberger J's analysis and conclusion in respect of the term "*a private dwelling house*" and confirmed that he saw no reason to differ from Neuberger J's conclusions on the issue.

A similar clause was subsequently considered in ***Wayne Martin v David Wilson Homes Limited*** [2004] **EWCA Civ 1027**. In that case, Buxton LJ indicated that:

(1) The question of whether such a provision limits the number of buildings which can be erected involves considering the clause in the context of the conveyance as a whole

(2) The use of the indefinite article "*a*" did not itself carry any implication of singularity;

(3) From a drafting perspective, if the draftsman wanted to limit construction to one dwellinghouse, it was said that: "*he should put that clause separately in the covenants from the user clauses. Secondly, he would have to refer to the erection of one dwelling house only, not to the use of buildings, extant or to be built. Third, he would not refer to the use of buildings in the plural*".

Covenants requiring consent

A covenant requiring consent may be framed in following terms:

> "*no dwelling house or other building shall be erected on the land hereby conveyed unless the plans drawings and elevations shall have been previously submitted to and approved of in writing by [the company/the vendor] but such approval shall not be unreasonably or vexatiously withheld*" (derived from ***Crest Nicholson Residential (South) Ltd v McAllister*** **[2004] 1 WLR 2409**).

The exercise of discretion under a contract was considered in ***Braganza v BP Shipping Ltd and another*** **[2015] UKSC 17** in the employment context. The decision has subsequently been followed in the property context, including refusal of consent by landlords under a lease: see, for example, ***No.1 West India Quay (Residential) Ltd v East Tower Apartments Ltd*** **[2018] EWCA Civ 250**.

The question of consent in the context of freehold covenants was recently addressed by the High Court in ***Davies-Gilbert v Goacher*** **[2022] EWHC 969 (Ch)**. The court summarised the principles to be as follows:

(1) It cannot be said that refusing consent is unreasonable simply because the concerns could be alleviated by imposing a condition;

(2) Where the objection to providing consent is based on aesthetic grounds, then it would not suffice merely to say that the proposed building/alterations were not to the taste of the covenantee (or others entitled to the benefit of the covenant) as this would be entirely subjective;

(3) In respect of the reasons for the decision, it was said that:

a. The court must make a finding on the reasons or reasons which resulted in the refusal of permission;

b. The process by which the reason was come to, and the reason itself, must be reasonable, requiring consideration of both limbs of the ***Wednesbury*** principle (see ***Associated Provincial Picture Houses, Limited v Wednesbury Corporation*** [1948] 1 KB 223);

c. A decision maker as part of a reasonable decision-making process must in reaching their reason exclude extraneous considerations whilst taking into account those considerations which are obviously relevant to the decision in question;

d. Simply because a consideration has been taken into account does not mean it contributed to the reason as a consideration can be given a zero weighting in the decision-making process;

e. Where approval is not to be unreasonably withheld and the covenantee refuses consent for a mixture of reasons, some good and some bad, where the result would still have been a refusal without the bad reasons then the result will remain reasonable and will not be vitiated;

f. It is not sufficient to say a consideration was taken into account – it must be a consideration which contributes to the reason.

When faced with a covenant which requires consent, it is important to address, inter alia, the following questions:

(1) Whose consent is required? Is it the covenantee or some other third party e.g. a surveyor? (see ***Churchill v Temple*** **[2010] EWHC 3369 (Ch)**)

(2) Can that person be located?

(3) Where the consent is limited to "the Vendors", do the prohibitions become absolute on the vendors' death? (see again, ***Churchill v Temple***, above)

(4) Does the covenant expressly indicate how the decision to provide consent should be reached?

(5) Is the consent provision framed by reference to reasonableness?

(6) What factors were considered by the decision-maker in reaching their decision?

(7) Can the party seeking to challenge the decision point to a failure to consider relevant factors or consideration of irrelevant factors? Did these factors influence the decision?

CHAPTER SIX

ENFORCEMENT OF FREEHOLD COVENANTS

Whilst there may be issues surrounding enforceability against the original contracting parties, practitioners are more likely to encounter enforceability by and/or against successors in title. In such a case, the following questions are likely to need addressing:

(1) Who has the burden and benefit of the restrictive covenant?

(2) What is the proper interpretation of the restrictive covenant?

(3) What remedies are available to the proprietor?

BURDEN AND BENEFIT OF THE RESTRICTIVE COVENANT

Burden

The burden of a restrictive covenant can never run under at common law.

The circumstances in which the burden of a covenant may be enforceable against successors in title in equity were recently summarised by the Court of Appeal in ***Bath Rugby Ltd v Greenwood*** **[2021] EWCA Civ 1927**:

> "*...But under the principle in Tulk v Moxhay (1848) 2 Ph. 774, a covenant will be enforced in equity against a purchaser*

of land (and other owners and occupiers) if (i) the covenant is restrictive in nature, (ii) it is made for the protection of land retained by the covenantee, (iii) it is intended to bind the land, and (iv) the purchaser has notice of the covenant (now provided by registration)...".

(1) The covenant must be restrictive in nature (confirmed by the House of Lords in ***Rhone v Stephens*** **[1994] 2 A.C. 310**). A covenant may be restrictive in nature, notwithstanding the fact that it is framed in positive terms. Accordingly, in ***Shepherd Homes Ltd v Sandham (No.2)*** **[1971] 1 W.L.R. 1062**, Megarry J held that the question of whether a covenant is negative is not a question of wording but of substance. For example, a covenant to pay would not bind the land: ***Greenhalgh v Brindley*** **[1901] 2 Ch. 324**.

(2) There must be some identifiable land that can benefit from the restrictive covenant and land that is burdened by the covenant: ***London County Council v Allen and Others*** **[1914] 3 K.B. 642**.

(3) The burden of the covenant must have been intended to run. However, note section 79, Law of Property Act 1925 ("**LPA 1925**") which applies to post-1925 covenant. Section 79 stipulates that:

> "*(1) A covenant relating to any land of a covenantor or capable of being bound by him, shall, unless a contrary intention is expressed, be deemed to be made by the covenantor on behalf of himself his successors in title and the persons deriving title under him or them, and, subject as aforesaid, shall have effect as if such successors and other persons were expressed. This subsection extends to a covenant to do some act*

relating to the land, notwithstanding that the subject-matter may not be in existence when the covenant is made.

(2) For the purposes of this section in connexion with covenants restrictive of the user of land "successors in title" shall be deemed to include the owners and occupiers for the time being of such land..."

As stated within section 79, the provision is only applicable where no contrary intention is expressed, for example where the conveyance expressly or impliedly suggests that section 79 was not intended to apply.

(4) In ***Tulk v. Moxhay* (1848) 2 Ph.** 774, the court identified the requirement to provide notice in order for the covenant to bind a subsequent purchaser in title. Such notice may be actual, imputed or constructive. However, since 1926, the notice requirement is largely satisfied through registration:

a. In relation to unregistered land, restrictive covenants are registrable under section 2(5)(ii), Land Charges Act 1972 ("**LCA 1972**") as a Class D Land Charge. Further, under section 4(6), LCA 1972 a restrictive covenant so registrable is void "*as against a purchaser for money or money's worth*" unless registered before completion of the purchase. Where registered, this shall be deemed to constitute actual notice: section 198, Law of Property Act 1925.

b. In relation to registered land, the position is governed by the Land Registration Act 1925 ("**LRA 1925**") which applies prior to 13 October 2003 and the Land Registration Act 2002 ("**LRA 2002**") which applies from 13 October 2003. Under the LRA 1925, the restrictive covenant was protectable through a notice on the burdened land: section 50, LRA 1925 (see also paragraph 1, Schedule 12, LRA 2002 for transitional provisions). Under the LRA 2002 a restrictive covenant is protected through entering a notice on the Charges Register of the burdened land (section 32, LRA 2002 and rule 84(1), LRR 2003). See also section 34, LRA 2002 for applications to register an agreed or unilateral notice on the benefiting land.

Benefit

Where there is annexation, the benefit of the covenant will run at law (***Stilwell v Blackman*** **[1968] Ch 508**). The Court of Appeal in ***Marquess of Zetland v Driver*** **[1939] Ch. 1** stated that such annexation will occur where:

(1) The covenant touches and concerns the land;

(2) The retained land must be capable of being benefited by the covenant at the time when it is imposed;

(3) The land which is intended to be benefited is clearly defined so that it is "*easily ascertainable*". The court noted that: "*The fact that the benefit of the covenant is not intended to pass to all persons into whose hands the unsold land may come is not objectionable so long as the class of persons intended to have the benefit of the covenant is clearly defined*";

(4) The covenantee and successor in title must have retained some part of the land which is said to benefit from the covenant.

As to whether the covenant "touches and concerns" the land or based on more recent formulations "relates to" the land, in ***Rogers v Hosegood*** [1900] 2 Ch. 388, Farwell J said that the covenant "*must either affect the land as regards mode of occupation, or it must be such as per se, and not merely from collateral circumstances, affects the value of the land*".

Further, in ***P. & A. Swift Investments (A Firm) v Combined English Stores Group Plc.*** [1989] A.C. 632, Lord Oliver indicated that laying down definitive tests were "dangerous" but that the following provided a "satisfactory working test" for whether a covenant touches and concerns the land: "(1) *the covenant benefits only the reversioner for time being, and if separated from the reversion ceases to be of benefit to the covenantee; (2) the covenant affects the nature, quality, mode of user or value of the land of the reversioner; (3) the covenant is not expressed to be personal (that is to say neither being given only to a specific reversioner nor in respect of the obligations only of a specific tenant); (4) the fact that a covenant is to pay a sum of money will not prevent it from touching and concerning the land so long as the three foregoing conditions are satisfied and the covenant is connected with something to be done on to or in relation to the land*".

It follows that, for example, a covenant that serves to extract payment rather than protecting/preserving the amenity value of land is unlikely to be regarded as touching and concerning the land: ***Cosmichome Ltd v Southampton City Council*** [2013] EWHC 1378 (Ch). Similarly, where a covenant is either expressed to be personal or the covenant indicates that it was designed to benefit an individual rather than being for the benefit of the land, annexation is unlikely: ***Sutton and East Surrey Water Plc v Kilby*** [2017] UKUT 248 (LC).

In respect of the requirement that it must be possible to identify the land which is to benefit from the covenant, the authorities demonstrate that even if a party shows an intention to benefit the land in question, this is insufficient unless the land is sufficiently identifiable. Accordingly, in ***In Re Union of London and Smith's Bank Limited's Conveyance*** [1933] **Ch. 611,** Romer LJ stated that, except in building scheme cases, "*a purchaser from the original covenantee of land retained by him when he executed the conveyance containing the covenant will be entitled to the benefit of the covenant if the conveyance shows that the covenant was intended to enure for the benefit of* ***that particular land***" (emphasis added). If, for example, the "benefitting land" is carved up into various parcels, one of the questions to consider before proceeding with enforcement is whether it was intended that the particular parcel in question was to benefit from the covenant.

The preference is, of course, for there to be some form of plan or map by reference to which the land in question is identifiable.

In practice, section 78(1), LPA 1925 is likely to be engaged when considering covenants entered into after 1925 and annexation is likely to occur by virtue of this provision (provided it is not excluded):

> *"(1) A covenant relating to any land of the covenantee shall be deemed to be made with the covenantee and his successors in title and the persons deriving title under him or them, and shall have effect as if such successors and other persons were expressed. For the purposes of this subsection in connexion with covenants restrictive of the user of land "successors in title" shall be deemed to include the owners and occupiers for the time being of the land of the covenantee intended to be benefited."*

Following section 78, Law of Property Act 1925, it is generally thought that annexation is easier to establish: ***Federated Homes Ltd v Mill Lodge Properties Ltd*** [1980] **1 W.L.R. 594.** However, whilst section 78 makes it unnecessary to state in the conveyance that the covenant was to be enforceable by persons deriving title under the covenantee or successors in title, the covenant must still be construed to determine whether the benefit of the covenant has been annexed, namely the land must be identifiable and the covenant should touch and concern the land (***Crest Nicholson Residential (South) Ltd v McAllister*** [2004] **EWCA Civ 410**).

If the requirements for annexation are satisfied, it will bind successors in title.

In equity, the benefit of a restrictive covenant can run where there is :

(1) Annexation, for which, see above;

(2) A chain of assignments; or

(3) A building scheme.

Chain of assignments

It may be that the benefit of the covenant has been assigned from the original covenantee, either once or through successive assignments. Where there is no annexation, a party may be forced to rely on a chain of assignments instead.

In ***Re Union of London and Smith's Bank Limited's Conveyance***, the Court of Appeal confirmed that: "*...an assign of the covenantee's retained land cannot enforce the covenant against an assign (taking with notice) of the covenantor unless he can show (i.) that the covenant was taken for the benefit of ascertainable land of the covenantee capable of being benefited by the covenant, and (ii.) that he (the covenantee's assign) is an express assign of the benefit of the covenant*".

The "ascertainable land" may be identified through the conveyance or transfer creating the covenant, any plans referred to in the conveyance or other extrinsic evidence (***Marten and Another v Flight Refuelling Ltd. and Another.*** **[1962] Ch 115**). On the question of assignment, in ***Renals v Cowlishaw*** **(1878) 9 Ch. D. 125**, Hall VC stipulated that any assignment need not be express but "*may be collected from the transaction of sale and purchase*" bearing in mind the purpose of the covenant and the extent of the land disposed of.

One of the practical difficulties which is most likely to arise is the ability to show a full chain of assignments, namely from the original covenantee to the person seeking to enforce.

Building Scheme

The circumstances of the individual case may allow for enforcement of a building scheme or what is described in ***Reid v Bickerstaff*** **[1909] 2 Ch 305** as a "local law".

In ***Birdlip v Hunter*** **[2016] EWCA Civ 603**, the Court of Appeal summarised the characteristics of a scheme of development to be as follows:

(1) It applies to a defined area.

(2) The proprietors have purchased their properties from a common owner.

(3) Each of the properties is burdened by covenants which were intended to be mutually enforceable as between the several owners, namely there is an element of reciprocity.

(4) The limits of that defined area are known to each of the purchasers.

(5) The common owner is himself bound by the scheme, which crystallises on the occasion of the first sale of a plot within the defined area, with the consequence that he is not entitled to dispose of plots within that area otherwise than on the terms of the scheme

(6) The effect of the scheme will bind future purchasers of land falling within the area.

(see also ***Elliston v Reacher*** **[1908] 2 Ch. 374** for a similar summary by Parker J. The decision in ***Elliston*** also indicates that the fact of a building scheme can be inferred from the circumstances).

Where there is no defined estate or clear intention for the covenants to be mutually enforceable, a building scheme is unlikely to be established: ***Livett v Hennings*** **[2022] UKUT 325 (LC)**.

Such a scheme may be evidenced through the conveyances, title plans, auction particulars (***In re Birmingham and District Land Company and Allday*** **[1893] 1 Ch. 342**), conditions of sale etc, although this is not an exhaustive list.

General points to consider

It is not always easy to establish whether land benefits from a restrictive covenant, particularly since the benefit of a covenant is not generally registered against the title of the benefitting property. Parties faced with such difficulties may make an application to the registrar to provide information about the history of registered title: **section 69, LRA 2002.**

A lack of sufficient information may also make it difficult to ascertain the risk of enforcement action and the extent to which a party should take out insurance in order to protect against the risk of enforcement action. However, any insurance should of course be properly considered in each individual case (and this may even be a requirement imposed by a lender).

Another point to consider is whether the "benefitting" and "burdened" land have ever been in common ownership. Any such common ownership extinguishes the restrictive covenant unless the common owner subsequently recreates them: ***In Re Tiltwood, Sussex*** **[1978] Ch. 269**.

INTERPRETATION

The usual rules on contractual interpretation are applicable when considering the wording and meaning of the freehold covenant in question. In the recent decision of ***Cheung and Infinity Homes & Developments Limited v MacKenzie*** [2023] EWHC 220 (Ch), Miles J confirmed that, following the guidance provided by the Supreme Court in ***Arnold v Britton*** [2011] UKSC 50 and ***Wood v Capita*** [2017] UKSC 24, the court had to "*decide how the words would be understood by the reasonable reader armed with the background knowledge reasonably available to the parties*".

In addition to what has already been addressed in this Chapter, one concern may be that the covenant in question is too uncertain and therefore unenforceable. For example, in ***National Trust v Midlands Electricity Board*** [1952] **Ch. 380**, the court was concerned with a covenant which stated as follows:

"*No act or thing shall be done or placed or permitted to remain upon the land which shall injure prejudice affect or destroy the natural aspect and condition of the land except as hereinafter provided.*"

In giving judgment, Vaisey J described this covenant as wide, vague and indeterminate. He proceeded to conclude that the covenant was void for uncertainty given that: "*the omission of any criterion by which these vague and uncertain words can be brought under some control is fatal to the validity of the restriction*".

REMEDIES

Generally, the remedies sought for breach of a restrictive covenant are as follows:

(1) Injunction;

(2) Declaration;

(3) Damages.

Remedies are further considered in Chapter 8.

CHAPTER SEVEN

DISCHARGE AND MODIFICATION OF RESTRICTIVE COVENANTS

Introduction

The law surrounding restrictive covenants aims to strike a balance between competing property rights. This often involves a tension between the right to have covenants enforced so that the character of an area can be preserved as against the right to develop and generate an income from one's property. The law recognises that, whilst a covenant may have been appropriate 100 years ago, the locality in question may have evolved to such an extent that the covenants serve no real purpose or place disproportionate restrictions on a person's use of their land.

Accordingly, section 84 Law of Property Act 1925 ("**LPA 1925**"), as amended by the **Law of Property Act 1969** and **Schedule 1 to the Transfer of Tribunal Functions (Lands Tribunal and Miscellaneous Amendments) Order 2009**) provides a mechanism for the discharge or modification of restrictive covenants in appropriate but limited circumstances.

Grounds

The starting point is section 84(1), LPA 1925 which provides that:

> "*The Upper Tribunal shall (without prejudice to any concurrent jurisdiction of the court) have power from time to*

> *time, on the application of any person interested in any freehold land affected by any restriction arising under covenant or otherwise as to the user thereof or the building thereon, by order wholly or partially to discharge or modify any such restriction…*".

It is important to note that section 84(1) refers to a restriction "as to the user" of the land. A restriction under a covenant prohibiting the registration of a transfer of a registered lease without the consent of the covenantee is unlikely to fall within the scope of this provision: ***Re Cammiade*** **[2023] UKUT 96 (LC)**.

The grounds for making any such application broadly fall into the following categories:

(1) The restriction ought to be deemed obsolete (section 84(1)(a));

(2) The continued existence of the restrictive covenant would impede some reasonable user of the land (section 84(1)(aa));

(3) The person entitled to the benefit of the restriction has agreed to the covenant being discharged or modified (section 84(1)(b));

(4) The proposed discharge or modification will not injure the persons entitled to the benefit of the restriction (section 84(1)(c)).

Obsolete

The question of whether a covenant ought to be deemed "obsolete" is determined by reference to "*changes in the character of the property or the neighbourhood or other circumstances of the case which the Upper Tribunal may deem material*".

The issue of obsoletion arises frequently (but not exclusively) in the context of residential areas where there has been some commercial development, giving rise to argument that the character of the neighbourhood has evolved and therefore further development should be permitted.

For example, in ***Re Truman Hanbury & Buxton & Co Ltd's Application*** **[1956] 1 QB 261**, the court was concerned with a restrictive covenant which stated that the "*trade of a hotel keeper, innkeeper, victualler of wines, spirits or beer [were] not to be carried on upon the said land*". Whilst the original intention had been for the estate to be residential, various shops had been erected. The applicant (a firm of brewers) failed to persuade the Tribunal, and subsequently the Court of Appeal, that the covenant was obsolete. The key points to take away from the decision (and which remain of importance to those advising on discharge) are as follows:

(1) The court is likely to consider the extent to which there is any value remaining in the covenants. Thus, a change of character is a necessary but not sufficient requirement when arguing that a covenant is obsolete.

(2) The evidence adduced should demonstrate that the restriction "*is no longer necessary for any reasonable purpose*" for the person with the benefit of the covenant.

(3) The purpose for which the covenants were imposed and whether that purpose can realistically still be achieved are highly pertinent factors.

(4) The section 84 grounds, whilst distinct, are clearly intertwined. Accordingly, where there is likely to be injury to those with the benefit of the covenant if it were discharged, this would support the proposition that the covenant is not obsolete.

Subsequent cases have applied (and to some extent) extended the reasoning in ***Re Truman***. For instance, in ***Adams v Sherwood*** [2018] UKUT 411 (LC), it was said that in determining the purpose or object of a covenant, one may look to the instrument imposing the restriction, draw inferences from the nature of the restriction or draw inferences from the "known circumstances".

Notwithstanding the difficulties with demonstrating that a covenant is obsolete, the Tribunal will (of course) be prepared to reach such a conclusion in an appropriate case. A recent example of where the Tribunal considered a restrictive covenant to be obsolete is the decision in ***HAE Developments Ltd v The Croft Ealing Ltd*** [2022] UKUT 120 (LC). In that case, the Tribunal was concerned with whether the following covenants were obsolete:

> "2. *There shall not be erected on the said land any building other than one dwellinghouse of brick or stone or of both materials with necessary outbuildings garage accommodation and greenhouses.*
>
> 4. *No trade or business shall be carried on upon the said land or any part thereof but the same shall be used only as a private dwellinghouse and no act or thing shall be done or suffered thereon which shall be a nuisance or annoyance to the owners or occupiers of adjacent land*".

In reaching the conclusion that the covenants were obsolete, the Tribunal recognised that various houses in the neighbourhood had been converted to flats and it was evident that the neighbourhood had changed considerably.

Reasonable user of the land

Modification or discharge is also permitted where (in cases where section 84(1A), LPA 1925 applies) the continued existence of the restriction would impede a reasonable user of the land for public or private purposes (section 84(1)(aa)).

Section 84(1A) provides that:

> "*Subsection (1) (aa) above authorises the discharge or modification of a restriction by reference to its impeding some reasonable user of land in any case in which the Upper Tribunal is satisfied that the restriction, in impeding that user, either—*
>
> *(a) does not secure to persons entitled to the benefit of it any practical benefits of substantial value or advantage to them; or*
>
> *(b) is contrary to the public interest;*
>
> *and that money will be an adequate compensation for the loss or disadvantage (if any) which any such person will suffer from the discharge or modification*".

In *Re Bass Ltd's Application* (1973) **26 P. & C.R. 156**, the Tribunal approached an application under section 84(1)(aa) using a 7-stage process: (1) Is the proposed user reasonable? (2) Do the covenants impede that user? (3) Does impeding the proposed user secure practical benefits to the objectors? (4) If the answer to Question 3 is affirmative, are those benefits of substantial value or advantage? (5) Is impeding the proposed user contrary to the public interest? (6) If the answer to Question 4 is negative, would money be an adequate compensation? (7) If the answer to Question 5 is affirmative, would money be an adequate compensation? This approach has been endorsed and adopted in subsequent decisions.

Section 84(1)(aa) uses the words "*some reasonable user*" and it is clear that this does not mean that the use proposed must be the "only reasonable use": ***Shephard v Turner*** [2006] 2 P & CR 28.

As to the question of whether the covenant secures a practical benefit of substantial value or advantage, the authorities indicate as follows:

(1) It must be shown that (were the covenant to remain unmodified) it would hinder "*to a real, sensible degree*" the reasonable use of the land, having regard to: the location, surrounding property and the purpose of the covenant (***Re Ghey's Application*** [1957] 2 Q.B. 650).

(2) The fact that the provision uses the words "value or advantage" indicates that the benefit should not be circumscribed to those which can be assessed in monetary terms (***Re Bass***). Thus, a practical benefit may include: the preservation of a view (***Gilbert v Spoor*** [1983] 1 Ch 27); privacy (***Re Henderson's Conveyance*** [1940] Ch 835); the maintenance of a stipulated density (***Re Saviker (No. 2)*** (1973) 26 P & CR 441); or overlooking/intrusions (***Creebray Limited v Dennison*** [2020] UKUT 262 (LC)).

(3) The words "practical benefit" are of wide import and may even include a view which is not enjoyed from the land of the person entitled to the benefit of the covenant (***Gilbert v Spoor***).

(4) The benefit must flow from the observance of the restriction rather than the existence of the restriction (***Re Diggens' Application (No.2)*** [2001] 2 EGLR 163).

(5) Where other developments, which are compliant with the covenant in question, would cause similar damage, a Tribunal may question the extent to which the benefit secured by a covenant is of substantial value. Much would, however, depend on "*the degree of probability of such other development being carried out and how bad, in comparison to the [applicant's] scheme, the effects of that development would be*" (***Re Fairclough Homes Limited*** LP/30/2001 referred to in ***Shephard v Turner***).

(6) In ***Re Falmouth Dockyard*** [2017] UKUT 0430 (LC), the application to modify was resisted by the proprietor of neighbouring land based on the potential impact on its business. The Tribunal concluded that the covenants in respect of yachts and leisure craft did not secure practical benefits of substantial value or advantage: (1) the objectors operated in the commercial and military markets whereas the applicants operated in the leisure craft market; and (2) the objectors had no future intention to compete with the applicants and, in any event, there were restrictions on the extent to which the objectors could even carry out such works. However, the restrictions on the applicants' ability to operate in the commercial and military market (in competition with the objectors) did secure practical benefits of substantial value.

(7) A covenant which restricted use to "*offices with ancillary residential accommodation*" could, in principle, be perceived as a practical benefit where it facilitated effective case management. However, where the benefit was of "*nebulous value or advantage*", this would not be sufficient to defend an application for modification or discharge so as to allow for use as a private member's club (***Berkeley Square Investments Ltd v Berkeley Square Holdings Ltd*** [2019] UKUT 384 (LC)). In ***Berkley Square***, the Tribunal rejected the argument that

modification of the restriction would have a detrimental effect, including diminishing the profitability of an existing private member's club.

In the context of practical benefit, objectors often advance the argument that modification or discharge of a restriction may essentially sanction further development and (as a corollary) alter the context in which further applications are made and considered. This is known as the "thin end of the wedge argument".

This "thin end of the wedge argument" has often been applied in the context of building schemes. For example, in ***Re Snaith & Dolding*** **(1995) 71 P & CR 104**, it was recognised that a successful application may lead to further development which would impinge upon a "*a carefully maintained and outstanding successful scheme of development*". In such circumstances, a person benefiting from a covenant may be deprived of a substantial practical benefit in the form of "*the integrity of the building scheme*".

However, the argument is not limited to such building schemes. Accordingly, in ***Re Diggens' Application (No.2)*** it was acknowledged that the avoidance of setting a precedent for future development could be regarded as a substantial practical benefit.

Alternatively, it may be that the restriction, in impeding reasonable use, is contrary to the public interest. The authorities demonstrate that the notion of "public interest" and whether it is engaged in a given case is essentially a fact-sensitive question. One example of a public interest may be the provision of affordable housing (***Millgate Developments Ltd and another v Alexander Devine Children's Cancer Trust*** [2020] UKSC 45).

The courts have provided clear guidance on how the analysis in respect of the "public interest" subsection should be conducted.

In ***In re Collins' Application*** **(1975) 30 P & CR 527** the court considered that "public interest" essentially meant that the interest was "*so important and immediate as to justify the serious interference with private rights and the sanctity of contract*". More recently, in ***Millgate***, Lord Burrows stated that a Tribunal should ask itself *"whether that impediment, by continuation of the restrictive covenant, is contrary to the public interest"*. This did not mean taking into account all the circumstances that may be relevant in addressing a wider (and incorrect) question of whether it would be contrary to the public interest to maintain the covenant.

Agreement

Section 84(1)(b) refers to agreement by the persons entitled to the benefit of the restriction to discharge or modification of the covenant. Such agreement could either be express or implied by their acts or omissions.

Injury

Section 84(1)(c) allows for discharge or modification where *"the proposed discharge or modification will not injure the persons entitled to the benefit of the restriction"*. The arguments under this subsection often overlap with the other grounds and so the same analysis may apply. For example, in ***Re Truman***, the court concluded that where serious injury would result from discharge, it was difficult to see how the covenant could be regarded as obsolete.

Injury does not arise where the objection stems from a duty or moral obligation (***Ridley v Taylor*** **[1965] 1 WLR 611**).

Where a restriction "*preserves pleasant views of the application land from the principal objectors' houses and gardens, preserves their privacy, prevents overlooking and proximity, maintains the status quo, including spaciousness and a density of one house per plot, prevents unsuitable backland development, prevents the setting of a precedent for future development and prevents nuisance and annoyance from building works*" modification to permit a development may cause injury to the persons entitled to the benefit of the restriction (***Re Diggens' Application*** *(No.2)*).

The specific "injuries" which an objector may suffer in a given case will of course vary but may include factors such as: overlooking/ privacy, noise pollution, congestion or cooking odours. However, it is always important to bear in mind the wording of the covenant and what it is designed to protect. If, for instance, a covenant does not prevent overlooking in any event, a Tribunal is unlikely to be persuaded by the argument that a modification which augments overlooking is sufficiently injurious: ***HAE Developments Ltd v The Croft Ealing Ltd.*** Conversely, where the wording of a covenant is clearly intended to protect overlooking, more weight is likely to be attached to any increased overlooking which is likely to emanate from a proposed modification or discharge (***Creebray Limited v Dennison***).

Discretion

Where one of the section 84 grounds are satisfied, the Tribunal has a discretion as to whether to modify the restrictive covenants or not.

In re Trustees of the Green Masjid and Madrasah's Application [2013] UKUT 355 (LC), it was argued that the discretion should be exercised against the applicants given that they knowingly acted in breach of covenant. The Tribunal stated that when a jurisdictional ground had been established, the discretion to refuse the application should be "*cautiously exercised*". Further, it was said that the discretion should not be exercised as a punishment unless the conduct was "*egregious and unconscionable*". The Tribunal exercised its discretion to modify, notwithstanding the fact that the applicants had acted in breach of covenant; specifically: (1) the applicants were charitable trustees who were using the property for religious purposes; and (2) the applicants had made the mistake of assuming that the grant of planning permission would be determinative.

Conversely, in ***Re Falmouth***, it was said that there was nothing within section 84 to suggest that the power is to be exercised cautiously or sparingly.

More recently in ***Millgate***, the Supreme Court confirmed that it is more appropriate for a Tribunal to consider the manner of the breach at the stage of exercising its discretion and not when considering whether the section 84 grounds had been satisfied. In that case, the developer had the option of building the required housing on unencumbered land which would, as a consequence, have removed the need for a section 84 application. Further, if the developer had applied under section 84 prior to commencing construction, they would most likely not have been able to satisfy the "contrary to public interest" ground. The Supreme Court stipulated that such "cynical conduct" was to be taken into account at the discretion stage.

Whilst ***Millgate*** was described by the Supreme Court as exceptional on its facts, it is apparent from the case law that the conduct of the applicant (including whether they have knowingly acted in breach of covenant) is likely to be considered when the court is exercising its discretion.

Relevance of planning permissions

Under section 84(1B), the Tribunal is to take into account: (a) the development plan; (b) any declared or ascertainable pattern for the grant or refusal of planning permissions in the relevant areas; (c) the period at which and context in which the restriction was created or imposed; and (d) any other material circumstances. Thus, planning permission is clearly a material consideration when a Tribunal is determining whether a covenant should be modified or discharged.

However, at the same time, it is important not to lose sight of the fact that planning decisions operate under an entirely distinct statutory regime to the LPA 1925 and so an affirmative planning decision does not necessarily mean that an applicant will be successful in having a covenant modified or discharged.

Accordingly, the courts have consistently indicated that planning permissions are not "definitive" or "decisive" but are relevant (***Gilbert v Spoor*** [1983] 1 Ch 27). Indeed, in ***Bell v Norman C Ashton Ltd*** **(1956) 7 P & CR 359**, Harman J was unpersuaded by the argument that social conditions which may require higher density construction could in itself override the sanctity of contract.

A developer who obtains planning permission to make use of land in breach of a restrictive covenant does not allow them to ignore the covenant (***Re Martin*** **(1988) 57 P. & C.R. 119**).

Compensation

Section 84(1) provides that:

> "*...an order discharging or modifying a restriction under this subsection may direct the applicant to pay to any person entitled to the benefit of the restriction such sum by way of*

> *consideration as the Tribunal may think it just to award under one, but not both, of the following heads, that is to say, either—*
>
> *(i) a sum to make up for any loss or disadvantage suffered by that person in consequence of the discharge or modification; or*
>
> *(ii) a sum to make up for any effect which the restriction had, at the time when it was imposed, in reducing the consideration then received for the land affected by it*".

The level of compensation in a given case is, of course, a matter for expert evidence. However, the authorities provide clear guidance as to the approach a Tribunal is likely to take as to the measure of compensation. In this regard, the courts and Tribunals have grappled with the question of whether compensation should be ordered by reference to a share of development value (***SJC Construction Co Limited v Sutton LBC*** **(1975) 29 P. & CR. 322**), diminution in value (***Stockport v Alwiyah Developments*** **(1983) 52 P. & CR. 278**) or some other method.

In ***Winter v. Traditional & Contemporary Contracts Ltd*** **[2007] EWCA Civ 1088**, the Court of Appeal discussed the extent to which the "negotiated share approach" (based on a hypothetically negotiated share of the enhanced development value) should be the proper measure of compensation payable under section 84. After reviewing the authorities, the court observed that compensation under section 84 was to be based on diminution in value or enjoyment of the objector's property rather than the loss of financial bargaining position. In determining this diminution in value, a Tribunal could consider the negotiated share approach but the percentage reached should bear a "*reasonable relationship to the actual loss suffered*". The decision in ***Winter*** does not represent a rejection of the negotiated share approach and there is still a place for such an approach where it is a fair reflection of an objector's loss.

Accordingly, in ***Father's Field Developments Ltd v Namulas Pension Trustees Ltd*** [2021] UKUT 169 (LC), the Tribunal concluded that a negotiated share may only be awarded insofar as it is the best or only way to value a loss of amenity.

Timing

An application under section 84 is typically made after a developer has attempted to negotiate a waiver or release of the covenants in question.

Further, given that section 84(1B) refers to "*the development plan and any declared or ascertainable pattern for the grant or refusal of planning permissions*", it would be more prudent for applications to be made after the requisite planning permission has been sought and obtained.

Whilst, in some cases, developers have brought a section 84 application after completing works, such an approach has been criticised by the Tribunals and courts: see, for example, ***Millgate Developments Ltd.***

Evidence and Procedure

Part 6 of the Tribunal Procedure (Upper Tribunal)(Lands Chamber) Rules 2010 governs applications made under section 84. The Rules cover, inter alia, the following:

(1) The procedure for making an application, what an application must contain and the documents to be provided with the application (Rule 32).

(2) The procedure for objecting and the requirements for any notice of objection (Rule 34).

The evidence which is likely to be presented to the Tribunal will, of course, vary based on the ground(s) relied upon and the discharge or modification sought. However, evidence will typically comprise of:

(1) Ordnance Survey maps;

(2) Any relevant planning applications/permissions;

(3) Reports on development densities and development patterns;

(4) Development plans and policies;

(5) A Tribunal's site inspection;

(6) Valuation evidence;

(7) Any expert evidence on the environmental impact of the proposed development.

CHAPTER EIGHT

REMEDIES

RESTRICTIVE COVENANTS

Injunction

The usual remedy sought and granted for breach of a restrictive covenant is an injunction.

The court may grant an injunction "*in all cases in which it appears to the court to be just and convenient to do so*" (**section 37, Senior Courts Act 1981**). For the powers available to the County Court, see **section 38, County Courts Act 1984**.

In ***Priyanka Shipping Ltd v Glory Bulk Carriers Pte Ltd*** [2019] **EWHC 2804 (Comm)**, David Edwards QC sitting as a deputy High Court judge identified the principles that apply when considering enforcement by way of injunction. In summary, he stated that:

(1) Negative covenants are ordinarily enforced by an injunction;

(2) It was not a precondition to enforcement by injunction that the party seeking the injunction should prove that it would otherwise suffer damage;

(3) An injunction is a discretionary remedy;

(4) Whilst injunctions are in the discretion of the court, such an injunction is likely to be refused where granting the injunction would be unconscionable or oppressive;

(5) Inconvenience or hardship were not sufficient reasons to refuse an injunction; and

(6) The burden lies on the party bound by the negative covenant to show why the covenant should not be enforced by injunction.

Such an injunction may be mandatory in nature, for instance where a dwelling or outhouse has been constructed in breach of covenant, and require the offending structure to be pulled down: see, for example, ***Wakeham v Wood* (1982) 43 P. & C.R. 40**. Nonetheless, much will depend on the circumstances of the individual case. A court may conclude that it would be unconscionable for a proprietor to rely on their strict legal rights where they are aware of their rights but nevertheless acquiesce when an offending structure is being erected: ***Gafford v Graham and Another*** (1999) 77 P. & C.R. 73.

Practitioners may also have to consider whether an interim injunction is appropriate in the individual case. The principles elucidated in ***American Cyanamid Co (No 1) v Ethicon Ltd*** [1975] **UKHL 1** will, of course, be applied by the court in determining whether to grant the injunction. The fact that the claimant may be seeking an injunction as a <u>final</u> remedy does not in itself mean that an interim injunction should also be applied for – indeed different tests apply. However, the failure to apply for an interim injunction may influence a court's decision on whether a final injunction would be oppressive: ***Beaumont Business Centres Ltd v Florala Properties Ltd*** [2020] EWHC 550 (Ch).

It is also important to establish whether any of the usual bars on equitable relief e.g. laches, acquiescence etc are applicable and the extent to which this will impact upon any claims for an injunction.

As to whether the court has the power to grant an injunction which does not relate to a cause of action in the proceedings, see ***Linemile Properties Ltd v Plater*** [2023] **EWHC 810** (**Ch**) where Sweeting J suggested a flexible and pragmatic approach.

Damages in lieu of an injunction

The court may conclude, for example, that it is oppressive to grant an injunction and therefore determines that it is appropriate to instead award damages in lieu. This is reflected in **section 50, Senior Courts Act 1981**, which provides as follows:

"*Where the Court of Appeal or the High Court has jurisdiction to entertain an application for an injunction or specific performance, it may award damages in addition to, or in substitution for, an injunction or specific performance*".

The power to award damages in lieu is distinct from any right to damages pursuant to the common law.

In ***Shelfer v City of London Electric Lighting Co*** [1895] **1 Ch 287**, Smith LJ provided a "good working rule" as to the circumstances in which damages may be awarded in lieu of an injunction, namely:

(1) The injury to the Claimant's legal rights is small;

(2) The injury can be estimated in money;

(3) The injury can be adequately compensated by a small money payment; and

(4) It would be oppressive to the Defendant to grant an injunction.

Shelfer was considered by the Supreme Court in ***Coventry v Lawrence* [2014] UKSC 13** where their Lordships were divided on the role that ***Shelfer*** should continue to play:

(1) Lord Neuberger stated that a "mechanical application" of ***Shelfer*** and an approach which involves damages being awarded only in "very exceptional circumstances" was wrong in principle and there was a serious risk of such an approach going wrong in practice. He further indicated that: (a) the court's discretionary power should not be fettered; (b) it would, in the absence of additional relevant circumstances pointing the other way, normally be right to refuse an injunction if the four tests were satisfied; and (c) The fact that those tests are not all satisfied does not mean that an injunction should be granted. Factors such as the public interest and planning permission would be relevant.

(2) Lord Sumption considered ***Shelfer*** to be "out of date" and that there was much to be said for the view that damages were ordinarily an adequate remedy in nuisance. Lord Clarke agreed that ***Shelfer*** was outdated.

(3) Lord Mance was not persuaded that damages would ordinarily be an adequate remedy in nuisance or that an injunction should not usually be granted in a case where it is likely that conflicting interests are engaged other than the parties' interests.

(4) Lord Carnwath agreed that the courts should move away from the strict criteria in ***Shelfer***.

Since ***Coventry v Lawrence***, the courts have tended to prefer the approach of Lord Neuberger: ***Beaumont Business Centres Limited v Florala Properties Limited*: [2020] EWHC 550 (Ch)**. It therefore follows that ***Shelfer*** remains relevant when considering and advising on whether the court is likely to award damages in lieu of an injunction.

Where the court concludes that it is appropriate to order damages in lieu of an injunction, the question then arises as to how such damages should be measured. In ***Coventry v Lawrence***, Lord Neuberger stated that the damages should not necessarily be limited to the diminution in value. He commented that "*the damages might well, at least where it was appropriate, also include the loss of the claimant's ability to enforce her rights, which may often be assessed by reference to the benefit to the defendant of not suffering an injunction*". However, he acknowledged that the court had not heard full argument on the point and therefore it was not appropriate to resolve this point. Similarly, Lord Clarke preferred to leave open the question of how damages should be assessed.

The court may award damages based on what a party may have been prepared to accept as a quid pro quo for relaxing the covenant:

(1) This was formerly known as Wrotham Park damages following the decision in ***Wrotham Park Estate Co. Ltd. v Parkside Homes Ltd. and Others*** [1974] 1 WLR 798.

(2) The position in respect of such damages was reconsidered by the Supreme Court in ***One Step (Support) Ltd v Morris-Garner*** [2018] UKSC 20. The court accepted that "negotiating damages" were available in circumstances where "*the loss for which compensation is due is the economic value of the right which has been breached, considered as an asset*". Further, it was said that such a valuation could be ascertained "*by reference to the amount which the claimant might reasonably have demanded as a quid pro quo for the relaxation of the obligation in question*"

(3) The sum is usually arrived at through considering "*negotiations between the parties had each been making reasonable use of their respective bargaining positions without holding out for unreasonable amounts*": ***Amec Developments Ltd v Jury's Hotel Management (UK) Ltd*** **[2000] EWHC Ch 454.** In that case, it was further confirmed that the analysis involved having regard to the cost or detriment to the claimant and the benefits to the defendant.

(4) Any profit which is likely to be made is likely to be referred to when determining a fair price for the notional licence: ***Severn Trent Water Ltd v Barnes*** **[2004] EWCA Civ 570.**

(5) The court will also consider, in the context of a hypothetical negotiation, any alternative possibilities available to the Defendant: ***Enfield LBC v Outdoor Plus Ltd*** **[2012] EWCA Civ 608.**

Declaration

A party may seek a declaration, which can be particularly useful in providing clarity and certainty for the parties going forward.

In ***Rolls-Royce Plc v Unite the Union*** **[2010] 1 W.L.R. 318**, Aikens LJ summarised the principles in respect of the grant of a declaration. At [120] he stated that:

> *"(1) The power of the court to grant declaratory relief is discretionary.*
>
> *(2) There must, in general, be a real and present dispute between the parties before the court as to the existence or extent of a legal right between them. However, the*

claimant does not need to have a present cause of action against the defendant.

(3) Each party must, in general, be affected by the court's determination of the issues concerning the legal right in question.

(4) The fact that the claimant is not a party to the relevant contract in respect of which a declaration is sought is not fatal to an application for a declaration, provided that it is directly affected by the issue; (in this respect the cases have undoubtedly "moved on" from Meadows).

(5) The court will be prepared to give declaratory relief in respect of a "friendly action" or where there is an "academic question" if all parties so wish, even on "private law" issues. This may particularly be so if it is a "test case", or it may affect a significant number of other cases, and it is in the public interest to decide the issue concerned.

(6) However, the court must be satisfied that all sides of the argument will be fully and properly put. It must therefore ensure that all those affected are either before it or will have their arguments put before the court.

(7) In all cases, assuming that the other tests are satisfied, the court must ask: is this the most effective way of resolving the issues raised? In answering that question it must consider the other options of resolving this issue."

Further, in the more recent decision of ***Poste Hotels Ltd v Cousins* [2020] R.T.R 31**, Morgan J identified that the court was concerned to see whether a declaration would serve a useful purpose **[99]**. Where the grant of any such declaration was not a "*practical or useful step*", a declaration was unlikely to be granted [**103**].

It is, of course, important for any such declarations to be carefully drafted and may, in an appropriate case, be drafted by reference to a plan or photograph.

Stay

A party defending a claim for breach of a freehold covenant may look to obtain a stay of the enforcement proceedings to allow for tribunal proceedings (generally in relation to modification or discharge of the covenant) to take their course first. This is permitted by section 84(9), LPA 1925 which provides that: "*Where any proceedings by action or otherwise are taken to enforce a restrictive covenant, any person against whom the proceedings are taken, may in such proceedings apply to the court for an order giving leave to apply to the Upper Tribunal under this section, and staying the proceedings in the meantime*".

EASEMENTS

Court proceedings

The remedies frequently sought in court proceedings brought for breach of an easement are:

(1) An injunction to prohibit any further interference with the easement;

(2) Declarations;

(3) Damages.

Injunctions and declarations have already been considered earlier in this Chapter and are therefore not repeated here.

Damages

Common law damages can be awarded under various heads, but most commonly:

(1) As compensation for actual financial loss;

(2) An award that reflects the diminution in value stemming from the interference (for which expert evidence is likely to be required);

(3) An award to compensate for loss of amenity, although this may already be reflected in any diminution in value damages;

(4) Negotiating damages (see above).

It may also be possible to obtain aggravated or exemplary damages in an appropriate case. See, for example, ***Perlman v Rayden*** [2004] **EWHC 2192 (Ch)**.

Recovery will, of course, be subject to the usual rules on the tortious measure of damages, namely remoteness, causation etc.

Abatement

Abatement is a "self-help" remedy pursuant to which the dominant owner can enter the servient land to the stop the infringement.

However, the right to abate should be exercised cautiously. Significantly, in ***Burton v Winters*** [1993] **1 W.L.R. 1077**, the Court of Appeal emphasised that: "*Self-redress is a summary remedy, which is justified only in clear and simple cases, or in an emergency. Where a plaintiff has applied for a mandatory injunction and failed, the sole justification for a summary remedy has gone.*" It therefore follows that abatement is unlikely to be appropriate in most cases given that:

(1) The question of whether the facts in question present a "*clear and simple*" case may not be easy to ascertain at the outset. In any event, the first step is generally to write to the party in breach, requesting that the infringement cease. It will usually become apparent at this stage what the arguments are (at least at a basic level).

(2) As indicated in ***Burton***, abatement is not available where a claimant has applied for a mandatory injunction and failed.

(3) A claimant is unlikely to want to risk an argument that they have caused damage or that the right to abate has been wrongly exercised.

MORE BOOKS BY
LAW BRIEF PUBLISHING

A selection of our other titles available now:-

'A Practical Guide to Estate Administration and Crypto Assets' by Richard Marshall
'A Practical Guide to Managing GDPR Data Subject Access Requests – Second Edition' by Patrick O'Kane
'A Practical Guide to Parental Alienation in Private and Public Law Children Cases' by Sam King QC & Frankie Shama
'Contested Heritage – Removing Art from Land and Historic Buildings' by Richard Harwood QC, Catherine Dobson, David Sawtell
'The Limits of Separate Legal Personality: When Those Running a Company Can Be Held Personally Liable for Losses Caused to Third Parties Outside of the Company' by Dr Mike Wilkinson
'A Practical Guide to Transgender Law' by Robin Moira White & Nicola Newbegin
'Artificial Intelligence – The Practical Legal Issues (2nd Edition)' by John Buyers
'A Practical Guide to Residential Freehold Conveyancing' by Lorraine Richardson
'A Practical Guide to Pensions on Divorce for Lawyers' by Bryan Scant
'A Practical Guide to Challenging Sham Marriage Allegations in Immigration Law' by Priya Solanki
'A Practical Guide to Legal Rights in Scotland' by Sarah-Jane Macdonald
'A Practical Guide to New Build Conveyancing' by Paul Sams & Rebecca East
'A Practical Guide to Defending Barristers in Disciplinary Cases' by Marc Beaumont
'A Practical Guide to Inherited Wealth on Divorce' by Hayley Trim
'A Practical Guide to Practice Direction 12J and Domestic Abuse in Private Law Children Proceedings' by Rebecca Cross & Malvika Jaganmohan
'A Practical Guide to Confiscation and Restraint' by Narita Bahra QC, John Carl Townsend, David Winch
'A Practical Guide to the Law of Forests in Scotland' by Philip Buchan
'A Practical Guide to Health and Medical Cases in Immigration Law' by Rebecca Chapman & Miranda Butler

'A Practical Guide to Bad Character Evidence for Criminal Practitioners by Aparna Rao
'A Practical Guide to Extradition Law post-Brexit' by Myles Grandison et al
'A Practical Guide to Hoarding and Mental Health for Housing Lawyers' by Rachel Coyle
'A Practical Guide to Psychiatric Claims in Personal Injury – 2nd Edition' by Liam Ryan
'Stephens on Contractual Indemnities' by Richard Stephens
'A Practical Guide to the EU Succession Regulation' by Richard Frimston
'A Practical Guide to Solicitor and Client Costs – 2nd Edition' by Robin Dunne
'Constructive Dismissal – Practice Pointers and Principles' by Benjimin Burgher
'A Practical Guide to Religion and Belief Discrimination Claims in the Workplace' by Kashif Ali
'A Practical Guide to the Law of Medical Treatment Decisions' by Ben Troke
'Fundamental Dishonesty and QOCS in Personal Injury Proceedings: Law and Practice' by Jake Rowley
'A Practical Guide to the Law in Relation to School Exclusions' by Charlotte Hadfield & Alice de Coverley
'A Practical Guide to Divorce for the Silver Separators' by Karin Walker
'The Right to be Forgotten – The Law and Practical Issues' by Melissa Stock
'A Practical Guide to Planning Law and Rights of Way in National Parks, the Broads and AONBs' by James Maurici QC, James Neill et al
'A Practical Guide to Election Law' by Tom Tabori
'A Practical Guide to the Law in Relation to Surrogacy' by Andrew Powell
'A Practical Guide to Claims Arising from Fatal Accidents – 2nd Edition' by James Patience
'A Practical Guide to the Ownership of Employee Inventions – From Entitlement to Compensation' by James Tumbridge & Ashley Roughton
'A Practical Guide to Asbestos Claims' by Jonathan Owen & Gareth McAloon
'A Practical Guide to Stamp Duty Land Tax in England and Northern Ireland' by Suzanne O'Hara
'A Practical Guide to the Law of Farming Partnerships' by Philip Whitcomb
'Covid-19, Homeworking and the Law – The Essential Guide to Employment and GDPR Issues' by Forbes Solicitors
'Covid-19 and Criminal Law – The Essential Guide' by Ramya Nagesh

'Covid-19 and Family Law in England and Wales – The Essential Guide' by Safda Mahmood
'A Practical Guide to the Law of Unlawful Eviction and Harassment – 2nd Edition' by Stephanie Lovegrove
'Covid-19, Brexit and the Law of Commercial Leases – The Essential Guide' by Mark Shelton
'A Practical Guide to Costs in Personal Injury Claims – 2nd Edition' by Matthew Hoe
'A Practical Guide to the General Data Protection Regulation (GDPR) – 2nd Edition' by Keith Markham
'Ellis on Credit Hire – Sixth Edition' by Aidan Ellis & Tim Kevan
'A Practical Guide to Working with Litigants in Person and McKenzie Friends in Family Cases' by Stuart Barlow
'Protecting Unregistered Brands: A Practical Guide to the Law of Passing Off' by Lorna Brazell
'A Practical Guide to Secondary Liability and Joint Enterprise Post-Jogee' by Joanne Cecil & James Mehigan
'A Practical Guide to the Pre-Action RTA Claims Protocol for Personal Injury Lawyers' by Antonia Ford
'A Practical Guide to Neighbour Disputes and the Law' by Alexander Walsh
'A Practical Guide to Forfeiture of Leases' by Mark Shelton
'A Practical Guide to Coercive Control for Legal Practitioners and Victims' by Rachel Horman
'A Practical Guide to Rights Over Airspace and Subsoil' by Daniel Gatty
'Tackling Disclosure in the Criminal Courts – A Practitioner's Guide' by Narita Bahra QC & Don Ramble
'A Practical Guide to the Law of Driverless Cars – Second Edition' by Alex Glassbrook, Emma Northey & Scarlett Milligan
'A Practical Guide to TOLATA Claims' by Greg Williams
'A Practical Guide to Elderly Law – 2nd Edition' by Justin Patten
'A Practical Guide to Responding to Housing Disrepair and Unfitness Claims' by Iain Wightwick
'A Practical Guide to the Construction and Rectification of Wills and Trust Instruments' by Edward Hewitt
'A Practical Guide to the Law of Bullying and Harassment in the Workplace' by Philip Hyland

'How to Be a Freelance Solicitor: A Practical Guide to the SRA-Regulated Freelance Solicitor Model' by Paul Bennett
'A Practical Guide to Prison Injury Claims' by Malcolm Johnson
'A Practical Guide to the Small Claims Track - 2nd Edition' by Dominic Bright
'A Practical Guide to Advising Clients at the Police Station' by Colin Stephen McKeown-Beaumont
'A Practical Guide to Antisocial Behaviour Injunctions' by Iain Wightwick
'Practical Mediation: A Guide for Mediators, Advocates, Advisers, Lawyers, and Students in Civil, Commercial, Business, Property, Workplace, and Employment Cases' by Jonathan Dingle with John Sephton
'The Mini-Pupillage Workbook' by David Boyle
'A Practical Guide to Crofting Law' by Brian Inkster
'A Practical Guide to Spousal Maintenance' by Liz Cowell
'A Practical Guide to the Law of Domain Names and Cybersquatting' by Andrew Clemson
'A Practical Guide to the Law of Gender Pay Gap Reporting' by Harini Iyengar
'NHS Whistleblowing and the Law' by Joseph England
'Employment Law and the Gig Economy' by Nigel Mackay & Annie Powell
'A Practical Guide to Noise Induced Hearing Loss (NIHL) Claims' by Andrew Mckie, Ian Skeate, Gareth McAloon
'An Introduction to Beauty Negligence Claims – A Practical Guide for the Personal Injury Practitioner' by Greg Almond
'Intercompany Agreements for Transfer Pricing Compliance' by Paul Sutton
'Zen and the Art of Mediation' by Martin Plowman
'A Practical Guide to the SRA Principles, Individual and Law Firm Codes of Conduct 2019 – What Every Law Firm Needs to Know' by Paul Bennett
'A Practical Guide to Adoption for Family Lawyers' by Graham Pegg
'A Practical Guide to Industrial Disease Claims' by Andrew Mckie & Ian Skeate
'A Practical Guide to Redundancy' by Philip Hyland
'A Practical Guide to Vicarious Liability' by Mariel Irvine
'A Practical Guide to Applications for Landlord's Consent and Variation of Leases' by Mark Shelton
'A Practical Guide to Relief from Sanctions Post-Mitchell and Denton' by Peter Causton

'A Practical Guide to Equity Release for Advisors' by Paul Sams
'A Practical Guide to Financial Services Claims' by Chris Hegarty
'The Law of Houses in Multiple Occupation: A Practical Guide to HMO Proceedings' by Julian Hunt
'Occupiers, Highways and Defective Premises Claims: A Practical Guide Post-Jackson – 2nd Edition' by Andrew Mckie
'A Practical Guide to Financial Ombudsman Service Claims' by Adam Temple & Robert Scrivenor
'A Practical Guide to Advising Schools on Employment Law' by Jonathan Holden
'A Practical Guide to Running Housing Disrepair and Cavity Wall Claims: 2nd Edition' by Andrew Mckie & Ian Skeate
'A Practical Guide to Holiday Sickness Claims – 2nd Edition' by Andrew Mckie & Ian Skeate
'Arguments and Tactics for Personal Injury and Clinical Negligence Claims' by Dorian Williams
'A Practical Guide to Drone Law' by Rufus Ballaster, Andrew Firman, Eleanor Clot
'A Practical Guide to Compliance for Personal Injury Firms Working With Claims Management Companies' by Paul Bennett
'RTA Allegations of Fraud in a Post-Jackson Era: The Handbook – 2nd Edition' by Andrew Mckie
'RTA Personal Injury Claims: A Practical Guide Post-Jackson' by Andrew Mckie
'On Experts: CPR35 for Lawyers and Experts' by David Boyle
'An Introduction to Personal Injury Law' by David Boyle

These books and more are available to order online direct from the publisher at www.lawbriefpublishing.com, where you can also read free sample chapters. For any queries, contact us on 0844 587 2383 or mail@lawbriefpublishing.com.

Our books are also usually in stock at www.amazon.co.uk with free next day delivery for Prime members, and at good legal bookshops such as Wildy & Sons.

We are regularly launching new books in our series of practical day-to-day practitioners' guides. Visit our website and join our free newsletter to be kept informed and to receive special offers, free chapters, etc.

You can also follow us on Twitter at www.twitter.com/lawbriefpub.

www.ingramcontent.com/pod-product-compliance
Ingram Content Group UK Ltd.
Pitfield, Milton Keynes, MK11 3LW, UK
UKHW020148290926
15471UKWH00004B/751

9 781914 608711